SiReNS

A MEMOIR BY
JOShua MOHr

Two Dollar Radio
Books too loud to ignore

Two Dollar Radio
Books too loud to Ignore

WHO WE ARE Two Dollar Radio is a family-run outfit dedicated to reaffirming the cultural and artistic spirit of the publishing industry. We aim to do this by presenting bold works of literary merit, each book, individually and collectively, providing a sonic progression that we believe to be too loud to ignore.

TWODOLLARRADIO.com

Proudly based in
Columbus
OHIO

 @TwoDollarRadio

@TwoDollarRadio

/TwoDollarRadio

SOME RECOMMENDED LOCATIONS FOR READING *SIRENS*: While crying in a rehab facility's bathroom; On a beach, in the dark, using a lighter's flame; While getting a tattoo of an ex-lover's name removed; While painting the toe nails of someone you love; Pretty much anywhere because books are portable and the perfect technology!

AUTHOR PHOTOGRAPH→ by Shelby Brakken

COVER ILLUSTRATION→ by Haejin Park

Illustration used with permission of BuzzFeed

Thank you for supporting independent culture!
Feel good about yourself.

"For while the tale of how we suffer, and how we are delighted, and how we may triumph is never new, it always must be heard. There isn't any other tale to tell, it's the only light we've got in all this darkness."

—James Baldwin

SiReNS

For those of us who want to do better.

PART 1:
COLUMBUS & COLUMBUS

Prologue

IT'S SIX IN THE MORNING ON NEW YEAR'S DAY AND Ava cries from the crib, which means my wife says something to me like, "Your turn," and I say something whiny like, "Bottle, fine," and stumble into the kitchen and spill milk on the counter and don't wipe it up, leave it for later, after coffee, after caffeine makes my mind fire right. I tuck the bottle in the waistband of my drawers so I can hoist Ava up with both arms, and she says, "Let's play," a new phrase for her, and I carry her back into our bed and lay her in the middle and get back in myself, Lelo and I flanking her, the three of us lying like a happy family, and for twenty seconds that's what we are.

Then the numbness starts.

I notice it first in my right arm, then realize it's creeping into my leg too. *That's weird*, I think, *two limbs falling asleep at the same time.*

Soon there's no feeling on that entire side of my body, from shoulder to toes.

I shift positions, rolling onto my back, so blood can flow freely.

Five seconds. Ten. Twenty.

Still numb.

Fear spills out of me like the milk rolling down my daughter's chin. I shake my dead hand back and forth, back and forth, and say to Lelo, "Something's wrong," and she say's, "What?" and I say, "911."

She's to the phone fast and I roll over onto my stomach, a gesture that Ava interprets as an invitation to play and she's straddling my back and yelling, "Hop on Pop! Hop on Pop!"

My frantic wife doing her best to conjure the paramedics and me knowing beyond any doubt that the numbness will zip over me like a body bag and Ava keeps chanting, "Hop on Pop! Hop on Pop!" and I am crying uncontrollably, grieving a girl I'll never get to see turn into a woman and if this is the end of my life, I wish it had ended sooner. Wish I had died before meeting Lelo, before ever seeing Ava on the ultrasound, the size of an orange seed, our nickname for her until she was born.

I wish I'd never gotten sober, never tried to be a better person. Why endure so much harrowing improvement to die like this at thirty-eight years old?

When I was in kindergarten I stabbed myself with a pencil, on purpose, for no reason—one minute sitting in class holding the thing in my hand wondering what it would feel like to be stabbed, and so I did it, hitting my open palm with the pencil's tip, screaming and sobbing and bleeding, the teacher taking me to a water fountain to clean the wound and berate me, asking, "Why why why, Josh, why on earth would you do that?"

I still have the graphite lodged in my palm. I'm looking at it right now. And for the next 50,000 words, you'll be staring at it too.

1

BUT BEFORE ANY NUMBNESS IN MY BODY, BEFORE Lelo and Ava, I volunteered at a halfway house in the Mission District, teaching creative writing. This was about ten years ago, 2004 or 2005, while I was in grad school at the University of San Francisco.

Kae was one of my students at the halfway house. He had spent fifteen years in San Quentin and was out two weeks when I met him. One of the conditions of his parole was that he had to stay clean or he'd be busted back to prison. After the first session we had together, he came up to me and said, "Gonna be the first American Indian to win the National Book Award for nonfiction."

It made me like him immediately. Call it cachet, swagger. Here he was fresh from the penitentiary and he had no fear of odds, no concept of how remote the chances were of that happening. Or he did know and didn't care. Maybe winning the National Book Award seemed easy after pulling all those years in prison.

The first essay he handed in made me think he actually might do it. The scene was short, maybe four or five paragraphs that dramatized Kae sitting on the sidewalk, against the front of a 24-hour donut shop in San Francisco's Tenderloin District, the part of town where junkies roamed in an animal refuge, no police, no poachers, so long as they kept their chaos in a contained radius. This is changing as the city gentrifies, but back then, the TL was an addict asylum.

Leaning on the donut shop, Kae was out of heroin and he wore only an undershirt and he'd never been so cold in his life, so hungry, so depleted. A taxi parked out front of the donut shop, the driver talking on his cell, arguing with someone. Kae watched words explode from the driver's mouth and then he saw the exhaust puffing from the tailpipe, looking like a steam room, giving him an idea. Freezing, Kae crawled, pulled himself across the sidewalk to the cab's back, first warming his hands in the exhaust, finally submerging his head in that toxic cloud, lathering himself in the car's warmth and affection.

The story ended there, the reader sucking carbon monoxide right along with Kae, smelling the acrid poison, but also feeling its billowy tenderness.

I finished it and started right back at the beginning, reread it a few more times. This guy was good and needed help, needed someone to treat him like he wasn't just another convict.

"You might do it," I said to Kae, handing his essay back with my notes, ways I thought he could make it even better.

"Do what?"

"Win the National Book Award."

He eyeballed me. Kae was in his fifties, dark complexion set off with pale patches of eczema that he constantly scratched. His head was kept in a crew cut. Old and faded tribal tattoos on his forearms.

"Course I'll do it," said Kae.

———

They were always calling out, screwing around, and I dug their chaos during our classes. They didn't have to front tough; no one was a gangster while we wrote. Nobody had felonies hanging from their necks like nooses. We were people talking about storytelling, and that was all we were.

I even had one student who was illiterate. She came up to me and said, "Do you have to know reading for this class?"

She was in her forties. I stayed after our sessions and read our assignments to her. Usually, she didn't like the stories I chose, saying something like, "These people is snobs." She was right. My first batch of stories was too much head, not enough heart. All the characters brandished vocabularies like weapons, but all it really did for them was provide more words to describe their disappointments in life.

Everyone was in some sort of halfway house.

One time, I was scheduled to teach the morning after Valentine's Day. My ex-wife—well, she wasn't my ex yet when this all happened: Blue was still my disappointed wife, my why-did-I-pick-this-guy wife—decided that we should go out for a fancy Valentine's Day dinner. It was only one meal after all and what could go wrong?

I went from martinis to a few beers and we drank a couple bottles of champagne during the meal and don't forget after-dinner drinks. We had to cocktail hard, otherwise there was this whole conversation thing. Couples have to talk, they say. We hadn't been talking much at all because earlier that week we'd had a huge fight. I'd done another dumb thing so I bunked at Shany's house, making up maudlin and self-sympathetic remixes of what had happened. Shany was my best friend, and even she thought I was in the wrong.

"Have you even apologized to her?" she said.

"We both need to say we're sorry."

"So no."

"Not yet."

"If you want to fix this, go home."

So I slunk back. I don't even think Blue took her eyes off the

TV when I rolled in. Blue needed to believe in something and I wasn't giving her much. We spent pretty much every night in one Mission District bar or another. Hell, we had fallen in love in dive bars, but recently she'd grown weary of going at it so hard every night, which didn't make sense to me.

Weary?

Of what?

Of whiskey and jukeboxes and free peanuts? Of friends and adventures and bummed smokes? Of giving a kiss to an angel you'll never see again? Of all singing along when "Sister Christian" played from cheap speakers?

I'm not one of those sober cats who looks back and demonizes everything from when they were dirty. I'm glad I embarrassed myself all those nights because I learned what shame was.

What shame is.

It's impossible to describe real shame to somebody who hasn't thrived on self-destruction.

———

Kae wasn't having it. We met at a café around the corner from the halfway house, around 15th and Mission. Talking about his donut shop essay. I had made a bunch of suggestions for how to make it better, but he didn't think it needed any improvements.

"Already wrote it," he said. "It's done."

"You can make changes. Writers revise."

"That's the whole story already on the page."

He was distracted, looking out the window, scratching his eczema. I was mad that he wasn't taking this meeting more seriously. I didn't get paid to teach there, so I sure as hell didn't get any money for sitting in a café, listening to someone say he wouldn't edit.

"Are you waiting for somebody?" I said, knocking on the window.

He didn't even look at me. "Ain't got nobody to wait for."

"Your story is pretty good," I said, trying to make him focus, "but it can be great."

"Used to grind right down there," Kae said, pointing up 16th street. There was a BART station and everyone knew if you needed opiates or crack or crank in the Mission that was where you scored. I knew it intimately, buying bindles there myself, though I never told Kae. "Selling shit and getting high," he said. "How am I supposed to stay clean living a block away?"

"You do it so you don't go back to prison," I said.

"Easy as that, huh?" He still wasn't looking at me, staring out the window like he sat on an airplane and there was something panoramic down below, the Grand Canyon, the Rocky Mountains, heroin. "Most of my life was standing on those corners."

"Do you want to talk about your essay?"

"No," he said, "I don't."

———

Here was what had caused my fight with Blue earlier that Valentine's week: I was super coked up and had at least ten Fernets swimming in me when I met her and a couple of girl-friends (I'd been bartending around the corner and got off at midnight and hoofed to Laszlo) so we could all cocktail. I knew the guys slinging drinks there pretty well, Rick and Brian, who had a whole *Brokeback Mountain* thing going on, except instead of illicit fishing trips they blew dunes of coke and probably slow danced while the sun came up, much to the chagrin of Brian's wife.

Me walking over and kissing Blue and saying hey to her friends and immediately heading to the bar to buy the table a round, having a quick pop with the Brokeback brigade and striking up a conversation with the woman next to me, some debutante all dressed up, slumming it in the Mission, and I dealt with these posh ladies all the time on the weekends behind my own bar, as they turned our neighborhood into the Dirty Marina—the rich seeing how the paupers lived, or that's how it was back then; now the Mission *is* the Marina—and I hated these cross-town tourists but also dug making them want to screw me, and cocaine made me a charming chauvinist who some women found irresistible and apparently this lady was one of those because she flirted right off, and I looked her up and down and she wore these crazy jeweled shoes that looked like chandeliers and some belligerent carnival barker in my head demanded I drink whiskey from one of her chandelier-shoes stat.

Which I said to her, making her giggle and bite her bottom lip and I said, "What's funny?" and she said, "You're crazy," and I said, "You've got that right, pretty lady," and leaned down slipping off one of her shoes and my wife was at a corner table having no idea that I was being such a scumbag, simply chatting with her friends, waiting for me to come back with a round of drinks, enjoying a normal night cocktailing until the moment she couldn't stand me anymore, though that was still minutes away, me trying to convince one of the Brokeback blokes to pour whiskey straight in this girl's shoe and either Rick or Brian asking her, "You okay with this?" and she pointed at me and laughed and said, "He's crazy," and Rick/Brian already knew that, of course, and he poured whiskey in her shoe, my chalice, and the music thumped some Chicago break-beats, and most people at the bar started cheering when I brought the shoe to my lips and slurped out all the booze and the woman whose shoe it was clapped and made some sorority-style squeals and me asking the debutante if she wanted to dance and she said, "Sure," and I said, "Not here," and she said, "Where?"

I still had her shoe in my hand and I knocked on the bar with it and said, "Up there," and she squealed again and I jumped on the bar and pulled her up there too and we let the music take over, dancing terribly, me flying the shoe all about, doing my whole king-of-the-bar shtick, dancing with spirits and blow and a squealing debutante.

I wonder if Blue saw me herself or if one of her friends had to point toward the bar and ask, "Is that your husband up there?"

I wonder what went through her mind turning to look, having witnessed countless of my idiotic shenanigans, each of them tangling together, creating a huge ball of humiliations, too much for one wife to take and it was over, I was over, we were over, I'd gone too far not with the outlandish-ness of this one incident, per se—drinking from a shoe and dancing on a bar—but the speeding boulder of all the times I embarrassed Blue, and I bet she didn't even answer her friend, bet she simply stood and stormed and all the ire coursed through her and out her fingertips.

I never saw her coming, one second dancing and zooming the shoe in zigzags and the next feeling pressure on the backs of my legs.

Feet leaving the bar.

Weight flipping in a slow-motion tumble.

I must have dropped the shoe, must have brought my hands up to protect my face, must have thought it was the debutante's beau or a jilted one-night stand, it never occurring to me that Blue might mastermind this violent fate, still falling, still feeling my legs whipping up until I was upside down. I crashed face first to Lazslo's floor. Landed and lay there. And then it was like the whole room vanished. All the other people gone. Except the two of us. Blue and me. Music nixed. The shining shoe sitting on the floor. Blue standing above me. The look in her eyes was all anger. At this drunk she'd tethered herself to. At this person too dense to treat other people with dignity.

I lay there bleeding some and my head all sideways, shocked

but also proud of our life's chaos. Loved the shoves I never saw coming.

The shoe-chandelier should have been my headstone, a beacon, a lighthouse, tossing watts to mark the grave of a lousy husband. A whimpering eulogy flitting on the wind, saying *a parasite, a wrecking ball, a waste.*

———

Kae and I met before or after class for the next couple weeks. I'd worn him down about revision, about the idea that a story needs more work after its initial conception. I did this by sharing a couple of my short stories with him: I showed him the rough drafts, and then the final, published products.

"Which is better?"

"These is shit," he said, meaning the rough drafts. "These is solid," he said, pointing at the finals.

"So will you revise the donut shop piece?" I said. "I can help you publish it."

"Why do you help me?"

"I want you to win the National Book Award."

"I was playing about that," said Kae. "Can't win."

"You can," I said. "You're super talented."

Kae smiled. "You think?"

———

So on that Valentine's Day, Blue and I were stuck with wonderful French food in front of us and having a terrible time. She could barely look at me. From her perspective, dancing on the bar with that woman was the latest example of me disrespecting her. I had bad boundaries with the opposite sex. I knew it and she knew it and everyone we ran around with knew it, and that was what made her so pissed: how public it all was.

A couple free Fernets with the bartender on our way out the door. He and I had watched the sunrise a few times and told our war stories at mach speeds, all the cocaine making us sprint through our life's woes. I can't remember his name, but I can tell you his mom used to beat him with a hair dryer.

Blue and I were specifically calling it an early night so I could be semi-coherent at the halfway house in the morning. I had to be there at nine a.m., and I didn't want to show up stinking of booze. The people there worked so hard to clean up their lives, and I liked pretending that I was trying too.

But the cops had other ideas of how this Valentine's Day was going to end. Sirens and a failed field sobriety test. Blue taking a cab home and me heading to the drunk tank. Another night wedged in a cell with a bunch of hammerheads. The highlight was always a peanut butter and jelly sandwich early in the morning. Did I really like them, or is that only how I'm remembering it now? I remember those sandwiches tasting like they were made by god, the almighty creator sticking a knife into each jar, getting the proportions just right.

———

I brought a couple books that I thought would help Kae dig in to his rewrite. The first was Denis Johnson's *Angels*. The other was Amy Hempel's *Reasons to Live*. Those writers did emotional filth like few others, and I mean that in the best possible way. They'd be good role models on the page for Kae.

Somebody buzzed me in the halfway house and one of the supervisors called me into the office. She collated a huge mound of pages into a bunch of smaller stacks. She was fast at it. In another life, she would have been the most sought after dealer in Vegas.

"Kae got busted back," she told me.

"What?"

"He failed a piss test."

"So he's in jail?"

"In county now, then back to the pen."

"For how long?"

"For the rest of his suspended sentence," she said, not looking up at me, just slamming new pages down in her stacks. "That was a provision of his parole."

"How long is his suspended sentence?"

"I got no idea," she said.

"But it could be years?"

She actually laughed at this. "Oh, it's definitely years," she said. "Do you know what he did to get locked up in the first place?"

"Why?" I asked her. I knew she wouldn't be able to tell me anything, certainly not what I needed to hear. The information I was after could only come from Kae.

This wasn't the way his story was supposed to end. This couldn't be. I wanted to revise this part for him, re-imagine it from scratch, at the very least I wanted to highlight and delete anything about a failed drug test, about being busted back. That wasn't what life should hold for him. No, the first American Indian to win the National Book Award needed time at a writers' colony, not another stretch in San Quentin.

She stopped collating that massive stack of papers. "Why what, Josh?"

"Why did he relapse?"

The woman shrugged.

"There has to be a reason," I said.

"No," she said, "there doesn't. Happens every day."

She kept on slapping pages down on her swelling stacks.

I left the office and went into the room the students and I met in and wrote *Class Canceled* on the dry erase board. I stormed out of the halfway house and threw the books I brought for Kae in the trash. On the days I didn't have MFA classes, I tended bar at a place over on Valencia. I was scheduled to work that day but my shift didn't start for like seven hours. Time suddenly delegated to a wake, a funeral, a proper send off for Kae. If he was in his fifties, what, he'd get out again in his mid-sixties, seventies, not at all?

It made me think of him staring out the window of that café and saying, "Ain't got nobody to wait for."

And without anyone, he chose drugs.

I hit the closest dive bar and ordered a shot of tequila, a beer in a can; I made a cheesy eulogy-cheers for Kae and downed my shot.

"What's going on?" the bartender said, once I chugged the whole beer. He wanted to chum it up since we were the only people there. Without asking, he got me another tequila and Tecate.

"He's gone," I said and threw the tequila back. Kae had quit. He had one last shot to get his shit together, and he couldn't and all those years in prison that could have been avoided regenerated around his body, steel bars, cement, sealing him away from any future. If the stakes were that high for him, if he knew the skyscraping consequences and he still couldn't stay clean, what chance did I have?

Sure, I ruptured my marriage, but that was nothing compared to Kae or the others at the halfway house. Maybe I'd get divorced, fired. Neither of those offenses would lead me to San Quentin. Without any serious penalties, I was going to keep punishing myself. I don't mean with alcohol or drugs. It was never about that, really. It was the *punishment* that got me high.

Reminds me of a time in my early twenties, living in a punk house in the Sunset District, and I suggested a game of beer bottle baseball. I handed somebody a bat in our living room and stood like fifteen feet in front of him and I lobbed a beer bottle and he hit it and smashed it and shards of glass flew everywhere, including my face, cutting the shit out of my face, and I was laughing like the animals laughed, once they realized Noah's ark was going to float, and I kept pitching bottles and people kept clubbing the glass to bits and each and every cut on my face was where it was supposed to be, each cut was perfect.

That bliss!

"Another?" the bartender asked, probably wondering what was taking me so long with the new tequila shot.

"I'm going to drink so much I blackout."

"I've heard worse ideas," he said.

———

The morning after my failed field sobriety test, the heavenly PB&J, they let me out of jail about eight a.m. I had time to get to the halfway house to teach. I really wanted to go that morning. It felt important, doing something for other people.

I stopped by a store and bought a pack of gum and a bottle of Gatorade. There was no time to take a shower or brush my teeth. I knocked on the halfway house's door and somebody buzzed me in. The class started in two minutes.

The number of students fluctuated based on who had job interviews, who had to work, who had house responsibilities. The week before we had fifteen students, which was a record, and I thought the class was our best yet, and we'd build on it and things would get stronger.

Which made it even worse the day I came straight from jail. That morning, I walked into the classroom and no one was there. Not one student. It was nine a.m. and I figured I'd give them a grace period. We all need a grace period.

It was impossible that nobody would show. We'd had small classes before, maybe four or five. Never zero, though. That couldn't happen.

I sat there by myself until 9:30, and the only reason I got up was that I started crying. There I was, still drunk in the bathroom of a halfway house; there I was, the biggest wreck on the premises, and I didn't even live there. I had to get out. The longer I stayed, the better the odds that I was going to be discovered. Exposed for who I really was.

I heard Shany's voice saying, "If you want to fix this, go home."

"I don't know how," I said to the empty bathroom.

———

Me, you, any stranger standing around and watching, we would have messed up that morning at the donut shop. We'd have seen sadness as Kae crawled across the sidewalk to warm himself in a fart of carbon monoxide.

See, to Kae there was no tailpipe. No taxi. No driver. Kae didn't take in any of that.

He saw a house. Saw a mother making sing-song syllables to a baby in a bathtub. Saw kindness coming out of the exhaust pipe. Saw nourishment, grace, saw exactly what he needed to survive another day, and isn't that all any of us are after? Won't we do anything to survive?

There's no such thing as the long view when you're freezing, when you're broken. There's only the shortest path to the tailpipe. Life isn't about the comforts we covet. It's about the kinds we can crawl inside.

2

WHAT DO YOU STRUGGLE WITH—WHAT'S THAT one thing in your life that you wish to control, yet the compulsion spins constantly, relentlessly? We all have that seductive adversary, the voice in our head, calling us to calamity. What's yours?

Like Odysseus, and how he wanted to hear the Sirens sing: Everyone knew it was a death sentence. The Sirens were stunning women who lived on an island, and when sailors passed by and got liquored up on the Sirens' melodies, crews lost any semblance of themselves, abandoning their jobs, standing mesmerized and smiling at the voices while their vessels wrecked on rocks. Ships littered the bottom of the sea, all because of the Sirens' songs. No one ever heard them sing and lived to tell.

Until Odysseus.

He instructed his crew to tie him to one of the masts, fasten him so tightly that he couldn't break free. Then he told all of them to lodge beeswax in their ears, so they couldn't hear a sung note. He instructed them to sail close to the Sirens.

When their perfect, terrifying music began, Odysseus fought to free himself, ropes cutting into his skin, hurting him, but he couldn't care—it was the music, their music, a call to reach deeply into the heart of his world and jerk the organ out, stomp it to pulp. His crew, the Sirens' singing muted by the wax, navigated the ship safely. Odysseus heard their debauched propositions and lived to tell.

———

I'm thirty-nine now, writing this as a father, someone sober six years, writing this wondering if a look backward can make sense of who I am, what I am. Maybe writing this can make sense of my parents, too.

Because if I don't tell this story I might wake up in a week or a month or a year alone in bed, beckoning for my second wife and daughter, only to see them by the front door with their bags packed. I might have that mildew reek of a dive bar draining from my pores, might have shame snaking around my beaten-up face like smoke.

If I don't tell this, there's the chance I'll forget to fear my Sirens. Ava and Lelo will leave with their pulverized hearts and suitcases, slamming the door behind, but they might as well be closing me in a coffin.

———

Everyone said that our baby would be the best reason to stay sober. Intellectually, I grasped the concept and agreed with the sentiment. But to me, the baby seemed the best reason to relapse.

No one really talks about how hard having a kid is at first, everybody making it sound like a recurring miracle, each day an iteration of the same wondrous marvel, and maybe it is that way for some people, but not me. I felt trapped. It's being overtired, being on-call 24-7, being thanklessly worked, no seeable end to the madness, and all these things brought out the worst in my nature. They made me petulant, made me want to get whiskey and bask in beautiful failure.

I wanted a lurid, loud affair, not with a woman, but with a bottle, a baggie, a syringe. I wanted to check into the most squalid motel I could find and drink so much that I threw up. And then drink some more. Then do every drug. Then drink some more. And then let the next wave of alcohol poisoning spray out of me like a reverse baptism.

Jesus, how could I possibly want something so grim? I lived in San Francisco, one of the most enchanting spots on the globe. I was married to my second wife, Lelo, the kindest person I'd ever known. We had a daughter, whom I adored when she wasn't confusing the hell out of me.

There's that saying, *wherever you go, there you are.* I'd gotten sober, sure, but I'd taken myself with me, that fraction of my mind that worshipped ruin.

Even now, typing that line, I can feel it kick like a demented baby.

Saying, *hey stupid, let's be stupid.*

———

I still think about booze and drugs every day, triggered by all sorts of ubiquities. For instance, Ava and I play acoustic guitar together. I strum, and she sits on my lap, gnawing on the top of the guitar. Her teeth marks in the wood are some of my favorite things.

Every now and again she rips the pick out of my hand and tosses it inside the guitar. Now, there's no graceful way to get a pick out of the instrument, so I hold the guitar over my head, hole down, shaking it back and forth, the pick rattling around in there. And as it ricochets from side to side, I always think about pills. Yeah, maybe the pick has turned into oxy. Or Norco,

Codeine, Demerol. Maybe it's a pill and when it falls out I can gobble it up.

I never think it's anything else, while I shake the guitar over my head, listening to the rattle. I never think there's a penny in there. A glass eye. A nail. Never think it's a bullet. And I'm momentarily disappointed when the pick falls out, and I'm momentarily disgusted about that disappointment. And then it's over. There's simply a guitar pick on the floor. So what?

There are the times I make her a bottle, heaping formula into water. Invariably, some powder falls onto the counter and it's cocaine, and I want to line it up with a credit card, roll up a dollar. I have to feel that fiery high.

There are these triggers, and there are more, all the normal things that become drugs because that's how I see the world.

That's the guitar pick rattling around inside me.

———

Ava was born in the morning, and by the time eight o'clock rolled around that night, Lelo was out cold, exhausted from the difficulties of child birth. Ava was awake. I was awake. I sat with her in a rickety chair, next to Lelo's hospital bed, and read my daughter *Franny and Zooey*. I only expected to read her the first few pages, but she was content. I finished thirty, while she cooed and kicked on my lap. I read the next fifty after doing my first solo diaper change, a humbling experience. I woke Lelo for a quick breastfeed and after a burp, Ava and I returned to our lumpy chair—the place where I was supposed to "sleep"—and picked the book up where we left off. Ava dozed on my chest, and I kept reading aloud and finished the thing, sharing one of my favorite novels on her first day here.

———

A couple weeks after her birth, my mom and I decided to give Lelo a break—take a shower, take a nap, take a breath—so we bundled Ava up and put her in the stroller.

I was freaking out, wondering why I'd voluntarily ruined my life. What would happen if I dropped Ava off at the fire station's Safe Surrender Site? How angry would Lelo be?

That's the thing about being an older dad: You've engineered a day-to-day life that you dig, deriving pleasure from the narcissism of your routine. Since 2009, I had published four novels, writing every day and earning a living teaching other misguided romantics to churn out pages. I worked out; I traveled around doing readings; I spent time with Lelo, my best friend and favorite author.

During that walk, it was a nice day in mid-July. SF can be terribly windy during the summer, but it was calm, sunny. Ava cried in the stroller. Her squawking bothered me, but my mom told me not to worry about it, said she'd tire herself out and doze. In minutes, Ava did.

I pushed the stroller, Mom walking next to me.

"I keep crying," I said to her.

"That happens."

"I've made up these little lullabies for her and I can't get through one without crying."

"It makes sense."

"How do you figure?"

"You're in a new style of love," she said. "One you've never known before."

We were up at Holly Park on Bernal Heights. It's a small circular park that has a concrete walkway running around the outside of it and we pushed the stroller in this circle, doing laps.

"It's harder than I thought it would be," I said.

"Being a parent?" she said.

"I might not be able to do it."

"You're already doing it."

"That's not what I mean."

"It will get easier," my mom said, "and it will get harder."

"Super."

"Josh, she'll never know you the way you knew me," she said, stopping.

I stopped too; the stroller fixed in front of me.

"She'll only know you sober," she said. "Do you know how fortunate that makes you?"

"Who knows if I'll stay sober?" I said.

"Don't you dare."

"You know what I mean."

"Only sober: I wish that was how you knew me. Can you imagine?"

I didn't want to construct some fiction about our past, didn't want to worry about what had already happened. I wanted to stop circling the carcasses of all those years, which was one of the reasons I loved drugs in the first place: They yanked me into a paradise nude of memory. And it worked. Drugs helped me for years. That's what nobody tells you. Drugs help until they don't. But by then, you can't stop.

Nothing is my mom's fault. Sure, there's some genetic junk floating in me, unseen but dangerously there, like plastic in the ocean. But I ate that acid, smoked that heroin, shot that special K, bought those bindles.

My mom and I were still stopped in the park. A jogger whizzed by.

She had waited ten seconds for me to answer, and when she realized I wasn't going to say anything, she added, "Look at the baby," putting her hand on the stroller, right next to mine. "Just look at her."

Ava still slept, my three-week-old miracle, my three-week-old mind-fuck.

"She'll only know you sober," my mom said. "Just don't be stupid."

"Okay."

"As long as you're not stupid," she said, "everything will be fine."

———

But today... today is when my stupidness, my Odysseus, struggles so ferociously that he frees himself from the mast...

It starts like this: Ava and I are in the hallway, and I am locking the front door to our apartment. We live on the top floor, the third floor. It's an old building with brown carpet that looks like burned bacon. No padding underneath it. The white walls are barely painted, scuffed and gouged, modern art signed by the legs of bureaus, black scratches etched by tables' corners. But the apartments themselves are nice, only the hallways are a museum of the landlord's indifference. The best thing about our building is the smell: There's a laundromat on the ground floor, and our apartment is always perfumed by fabric softener.

Granted, that fabric softener's lovely stink is noxious and probably carcinogenic, but this is where we live.

Ava is jimmied between me and the front door as I fumble with the keys, as I'm loaded down with the diaper bag, our lunches, our jackets, she's fighting to free herself, and I say, "Hold on, sweetie, almost done," and she says, "No!" and I drop the keys, lean down to retrieve them and say to her, "Wait," and she says, "No!" and the diaper bag falls from my shoulder and Ava keeps fighting to free herself, and I say, "Please," trying to keep her wedged in front of me, and she says, "No!" and I work to keep her contained, to make this as easy as it can be, though nothing about this is simple, the ordeal of getting a kid out the door who doesn't want to cooperate, even when the destination is some place fun, some place she wants to end up, but the last twenty minutes have been a constant fight, "Let's put on your socks and shoes," and "No!" and "Let's get some snacks together," and "No!" and, to be honest, I'm wondering why I'm even working so hard to get out the door, lumbering us to the Peek-a-Boo Factory, which I know sounds like a German fetish bar with glory holes and adult-size changing tables, but in actuality, is an indoor play structure, basically a three-story hamster cage that kids can run around in and lose their minds, and she likes it, thus we go, that's the gig, that's one of the tenets of being a parent, putting their happiness before your own, so what if the Peek-a-Boo Factory is my worst nightmare, piping horrific music, all campfire songs sung by a gaggle of medicated children, the euphoric, most petrifying voices, timbres beaming and belting out cheery melodies, me trying to block out the accompaniment, yet it's not easy being in a hamster cage/insane asylum, one flush with a throng of hyped-up kids, with bored parents pecking iPhones on the periphery, using the Factory as a padded nanny, granting them an hour-long break from the day's barked demands for food and toys and the incessant messes accumulating around the house, sprouting up, seemingly spontaneously, *didn't I just put that god damn thing away!?* and maybe you did, maybe you didn't, maybe it doesn't matter because it's there again.

So:

My daughter doesn't dig running around the hamster cage by herself, no, she's a bit too young to want to venture into the upper stories without me, so I am forced to scramble around the cage as well, sweating and puffing and evading other children. I'm often the only adult hamster pushing past the padded walls, navigating up and down the narrow passageways, cramming my six-foot-two frame down on slides, between hanging plastic stalactites, etc, but a deal is a deal: Ava adores this, and I love watching her, each trip there revealing a new move for her, a new accomplishment, venturing into a small plastic room, sitting in there and clapping and laughing and looking at me and saying, "Echo!" and I lean my head in and say, "Echo!" and the first time she does the big red slide by herself, the first time she spins around on what can only be classified as a Sadistic Revolving Vomit Machine. I watch her do all these new things with each subsequent visit to the Factory and it's fun, if not a dash humiliating, but I'll embarrass myself day after day if it means being around her pure joy.

As adults, we think we know happiness, but all we really possess is a tangled, lodged remembrance of it, like hair in a drain. Being around a child, that's what joy looks like.

Today, however, we are far from the Factory. Today, we're struggling. Ava has been waking up at 4:30 for some reason, and about an hour ago I was so exhausted that I rubbed lube on my face instead of lotion.

So I'm down on the old brown carpet, on a knee in front of our apartment's door, trying to gather the keys and trying to hoist the diaper bag back up on a shoulder and Ava escapes my grasp and she's running toward the stairs and I say, "Stop!" and she doesn't answer, though I expect her to at least pause at the top of the stairs, expect her to feel an unconscious tug toward self-preservation, a fleck of survival instinct, but there is no pause, there is no acknowledgment of me saying, "Stop!" there is nothing but an eighteen-month-old launching herself off the top step and tumbling down the stairs.

Time does this odd division, in which on one hand, there's a slow-mo look to everything as Ava goes over the lip of the stairs: I see her head, her shoulders, her arms flap as gravity begins to take her down, it's anguishing, this swath of time, taking forever, and yet there is an assaulting velocity to this moment as well, her body moving away from me at mach speed, and maybe that's what this moment is—a slow-mo mach-speed movie—I can't move fast enough, despite the desperate commands screaming in my mind, *your daughter is falling, the person you're tasked to protect, the girl you love more than anything, why are you the worst, most worthless parent in the world with your kid falling down the stairs?!* and I drop everything, the keys and jackets and lunches and the diaper bag, all of it plummeting to the burned-bacon carpet, and I take two steps and follow her, diving down the stairs head-first, hoping I'm tall enough, hoping with my long arms I'll be able to snatch her halfway down, and I smash my knuckles on the banister and I feel a sharp pain in my balls, and I am as stretched out as I can, like Superman flying, though that's the shittiest simile I've ever conceived; there is nothing heroic about a hapless dad trying to right a situation that never should have happened in the first place. I shouldn't have been trying to do so many things at once. I should've put all of my cargo down, locked the door while holding her tight. I should've made two trips.

Poor Ava with the dumb dad sliding down the stairs with his bashed hand and hurt nuts and she's only three or four steps ahead of me, the carpet so trampled the floor feels like cement, Ava rolling down them, which is better than a head-first somersault-style plunge, her whole body hitting one step before flipping down onto the next; she has gone down about eight of them, she is making these noises—these terrible panting noises—and I can hear them—I still can hear them—each time I walk these stairs, I hear phantom pants, my little girl being injured because I'm too stupid to be alive.

Reaching my hand out.

Grabbing a hold of her thigh.

Stopping her.

She's safe, and I've saved her.

But too bad the human body doesn't have airbrakes. Too bad that a sturdy grip on her thigh doesn't trump the apathetic rules of momentum, inertia. Too bad that despite my best intentions we fall down the remaining three or four stairs together, roll to a stop on the landing.

Her wide eyes. The terror.

I can't smell the fabric softener.

I sit up and pull her onto my lap and check her little body, squeezing her limbs, combing over her head, looking for any blood, any damage, but I'm the only one bleeding, from my hand.

Then she starts crying.

Kids have different cries. *I'm cold* and *I'm hungry* and *my diaper is dirty* all sound differently from one another, various levels of anger and frustration and fear, but the one she wields on the landing is devastating music, and I'd listen to the Peek-a-Boo Factory's soundtrack everyday/all day so long as Ava stops crying like this. It's impossible for me not to hear one more voice embedded in her music, something subliminal, something only for me: blame. She can't articulate it but knows this is my fault. That's the dominant throat in this choir.

Something is really wrong with her. I know it. Internal bleeding. A broken bone. A dislocation. A traumatic brain injury. I remember reading about a child who hit her head in a bouncy house—a bouncy house!—and died, and if something like that can happen, there's no doubt that Ava is badly injured and it is all because of my incompetence and negligence and she keeps crying those desperate animal noises, and I grab my cell from my back pocket, and it isn't cracked or damaged, and dial 911 and I have to explain it, have to admit it, have to tell a total stranger that I let Ava fall down the steps and I begin by saying, "We need an ambulance," and she asks exactly what happened, and I say, "A child needs medical attention," and she says, "What specifically happened, sir?" and I say, "She fell."

Now a 911 operator isn't a priest, but I confess my involvement, trying to make her understand that I'm not one of those intentionally negligent parents, I am one of those doing-my-best-but-things-still-happen parents, I am a good person, though the world is a lair of peril, do you understand?

Ava continues to cry and kick on my lap, and I continue to

hope for an over-the-phone absolution, but all the operator says is, "Ambulance, on the way."

"We were going to the Peek-a-Boo Factory," I tell her.

"Would you like me to stay on the line until they arrive?"

"It's her favorite place."

"I can hold the line with you until emergency services get there."

"She loves it."

"Okay, sir."

"We go there all the time together."

———

Back about fifteen years, me and V: We had a platonic, polluted relationship, one running on booze. We both liked to blackout, dug talking shit and smoking cigarettes. We'd been in North Beach all night and now we walked to wherever we were going. I have no idea. Assume it was one of the bars on Columbus Street.

Let's talk about Columbus for a second because it had grown famous in our alcoholic circle because of Kerrie's ex-husband, Alan. Legend has it that one night Alan was wasted and called Kerrie begging for a ride home, and she agreed to pick him up, asking, "Where are you?" and he said, "I'm at the corner of Columbus and Columbus," and she said, "Those aren't cross streets. Where are you?" and again he said, "Columbus and Columbus," and that became a way to communicate when you were too fucked up to find yourself.

You were at the corner of Columbus and Columbus.

So that was where V found herself on the night I'm trying to tell you about. She staggered down the street and I was next to her, certainly not sober, but blocks away from Alan's notorious intersection. She staggered and then she fell.

Fell hard.

Right on her face.

Too blotto to bring her arms up.

She knocked out a couple teeth and badly chipped another. The blood seeped from her lips and she asked, "What happened?" and I wasn't sure how honest to be with her. I'd seen war movies in which one soldier, having just stepped on a landmine and missing both legs, asked another, "What happened?" and they said, "It's nothing serious; you're going to be fine."

I also wanted to comfort my friend. V and I waited tables together at this glorified diner and she was one of my favorites. At the end of our shifts, we had to put money in envelopes to tip the busboys, the bar, the hostess, and sometimes, we even left little envelopes for ourselves so we didn't drink all the day's take. We also had this fool-proof way of getting sympathy tips, if the diner was slow and we needed to maximize every table. We'd write thanks at the bottom of checks and spell it wrong— *thankees!*—and customers always coughed up 25%.

We might not have been soldiers risking our lives but we were human beings. She'd know the next morning how serious her injuries were. No reason to rile her up now.

"You're okay," I said to her. "We need to get you home."

Hailing a cab with a bleeding six-foot-tall woman under your arm wasn't easy. Several whizzed by us, and it became clear that I was going to have to work out alternative transportation. I threw V over my shoulder, giving her the fireman-carry. Like I said, she was a tall woman, really skinny, but still, she was heavy and I had a pretty good swerve going and periodically I needed to rest, keeping her over my shoulder but leaning on parked cars to give my legs a breather.

"Get off my ride," a guy said, coming toward us.

I understood his stance. I wouldn't have been happy either, seeing two heads on my car, but I was sure that if I explained it to him he'd calm down.

So I explained.

Yet he didn't calm down, didn't feel any human empathy, only saying, "I don't care… I don't care… I don't care… get off my car!"

Notice how level-headed I had been until this moment. This moment in which my friend was badly hurt. This moment in which I was only trying to get her home. This moment in which no cabs had the decency to help us. This moment in which I needed to rest my legs for like thirty seconds leaning on this guy's bumper and now he was screaming at me?

I folded V up on the guy's hood and squared up in front of him: "Here are your choices," I said. "I kick your ass all down the street or you give us a ride to my friend's house."

My hands up now.

Chin down now.

Getting in a boxer's stance.

Balls of my feet.

Bouncing.

"Just get off my car, man," he said, moving back a couple strides.

"We're past that."

"Just go."

"Give us a ride or we fight."

Nothing from him.

"Guess that means we fight," I said, taking a step toward him.

"Where do you need to go?"

"Only to the other side of North Beach. Over on Filbert."

During that car ride, he despised me but was trapped, seeing no other option but to play nice with his alcoholic car jacker. V nodded off in the backseat and came to every thirty seconds or so totally discombobulated and would start swearing at this guy out of nowhere, something like, "What the fuck is this fucker doing?"

"Shut up," I said. "He's helping us."

"He's a fucking fucker."

"Go to sleep."

"What happened?" she asked.

Then she'd pass out and the driver and I would look at each other, shake our heads. We had an apprehensive camaraderie brewing. I mean, he was only chauffeuring us because I threatened him, which is a precarious way for a relationship to begin. V would blip awake again, start with the whole spiel over: "What the fuck is this fucker doing?" and so on and we would have the same conversation, leaving me thinking that this was what it must be like to drink with that guy from *Memento*.

When we got to V's apartment, our driver peeled away, not helping me get her inside. I wondered what version of the story he was going to tell his friends when he got to the next spot. Would he change things? Make himself the hero? How he picked up a couple train wrecks stranded at the corner of Columbus and Columbus and basically saved their lives driving them home? Or would he exaggerate it the other way—that I was going to hurt him, that he met me, his near death experience, a psycho ready to tear into him for no real reason?

I mean, I might have.

There's no telling.

There's only conjecture—his story and mine—and I'm in the mood tonight to give myself the benefit of the doubt, something that doesn't happen too often around these parts. Tonight, as I puke this story up like I've got alcohol poisoning, and in a way I still do, I look back at these things and can say that I wasn't going to hurt the man.

And I mean it.

———

I scoop Ava up and meet the paramedics outside our building. I hold her while they check her out, bending limbs, checking eyes for a concussion, head for lumps or cuts, and one of them jabs me with questions re: how this happened, and he is a kind man, fiftyish with a white moustache with flecks of red, like pepper jack cheese. He is a parent, as well, three kids, and says to me, "We've all been there. Don't beat yourself up," but with Ava bawling in my arms, surrounded by emergency workers summoned solely because of my spectacular incompetence it's impossible *not* to beat myself up, though I don't tell him that, I only avert my eyes and kiss Ava on the head and say, "This is almost over," and their initial checks on her body reveal no obvious damage. They recommend that we go to the emergency room anyway, better safe than sorry and the like, loading the two of us in the back of the ambulance, me sitting on the gurney, Ava on my lap.

I take it as a good sign that they do not throw on the lights and siren, instead following the rules of the road like everyone else, and one of the EMTs gives Ava a brown teddy bear wearing scrubs, a mask covering up its mouth and Ava finally stops crying. She smiles at the bear. She smiles at me.

I say, "What's its name?" and she says, "Bear."

We do not know this at the time, but this bear will turn into one of Ava's favorite stuffed animals. She will carry it around for weeks, and it becomes some furry indictment, a denunciation in scrubs, every time I see that bear, I live that day, Ava jumping off the top stair, those harsh pants pushing out of her as she goes down.

Because she's so young, the emergency room is on full-alert, rushing Ava into an exam room with an army of doctors. I hold her on my lap as they give her a more precise check-up. Slowly, they determine she's fine, and docs peel off until it's only one of them. There's also a woman with a clipboard, who is here to verify/rate the verity of my story.

And she believes me. She even says that as a mother herself, she knows full well how these things happen.

She and Pepper Jack are so quick to offer pardons and I want to feel better, hearing their empathy, their grace, but I can't. I don't know how to buy "these things happen." They shouldn't. It could have been easily prevented. So stop giving me the benefit of the doubt.

I had called Lelo from the ambulance and now she comes into our exam room, very calm. Ava plays with Bear on my lap.

"Mommy!" she says, happy as can be.

"Hey, girl," says Lelo, picking her up into a big hug. "Are you okay?" Lelo says to me.

"I'm so sorry," I say.

It's my turn to cry. I don't know if adult-tears have various timbres and tells and queues like a child's, though I know that from the inside, this feels different. In that hospital room, a space allocated for examination, my self-autopsy turns up one fact: They're better off without me. I can't be trusted. I'll try to do the right thing, but I'll botch our life.

Lelo places Ava back on my lap, then she gives me a big hug herself: "Josh, it's okay, she's okay. Look at her!"

Ava bounces Bear around my stomach and chest.

"We're fine," Lelo says.

"Who's that?" I say, knocking Bear on top of its head and faking a smile.

"Bear," says Ava.

"Sorry we didn't make it to the Peek-a-Boo Factory."

"Bear," she says again.

——

Once I got V into her apartment, I contemplated putting her in the shower, but since she could barely stand up, why risk her falling again? So I stripped her naked and wiped her bloody mouth one last time and turned the lights out and she was in bed mumbling and cooing.

I stood by her bedroom door, eavesdropping while she talked

to god. Stood there thinking about how much of our lives we can dent and have no idea. No sense of the consequences till later. There was nothing really wrong in V's life yet. Not until she awoke the next morning. Not until she realized what had happened in her mouth. She'd stir and sense something was off. Something ached. Something was no good. And that was when she'd understand people like us made our own destruction. We suicide-bombed our own lives.

In that moment I wanted to curl up on her floor and be there the next day, to spare her sorting through the inchoate facts alone. So why didn't I? Don't know exactly—don't have a very good excuse—except to say it felt like an intrusion. Like I was barging in her consciousness, jumping on her brain's bed. It was her mouth and I had no right to trespass.

I still wonder about the specifics of the next morning. I've never asked her, don't want to make her hop in that agonizing time machine. She's someone I love unconditionally, and if it would have made it easier on you if I'd stayed, I apologize, V. I'm so sorry if I let you down.

We could have cooed to god together and maybe he would have taken mercy, a miracle happening before the sun came up. The tooth fairy coming not to collect your lost teeth, but to give them back to you, spackle them into your gums so we remained beautiful forever.

———

I can find some clemency and dollop it on the past, letting myself off the hook that night with V. I can say, *Live and learn*. I can say, *I'd handle it differently now*. I can say all those things and maybe they're true. But I'm impervious to all that about Ava's accident.

I'm sitting on those hallway stairs right now, actually, down on the old brown carpet, laptop balanced on my knees. There isn't an easy answer, and the only looping pollution in my brain is this: The world doesn't care about our best intentions; we will all be injured to varying degrees, we will all scar. I hurt my daughter and that's that. Another regret to add to the stash already ricocheting around my head like lottery balls.

Ava won't remember falling down those stairs. She's too young. But I'll remember it enough for the both of us. The longer my self-autopsy goes on, the longer I see Bear, its scrubs and mask, its muffled judgments, the whole scraping failure of Ava going down the steps, it all knots and swells and makes me want to relapse.

I walked away from V when she needed me. Maybe I'll walk away from Lelo, from Ava. Maybe I'll walk away from myself. Rationally, I know it doesn't make any sense, but I have a hole in me that can only be filled with liquor.

3

WHEN I THINK OF MY WEDDING DAY WITH BLUE, the first memory that pops in my head has nothing to do with her. I don't mean that in a disrespectful way. She was a gorgeous bride. But the first person I think of is my father.

He was a Lutheran minister and he performed our wedding.

Eight weeks later, he was dead. Stage four lung cancer.

So when most couples are in the honeymoon phase of a new marriage, I was grieving. I was grieving and drinking, making things so much harder than they needed to be.

Of course, I didn't know anything about that on my actual wedding day. I knew he was sick. Knew his condition was getting worse. But I tried keeping all that reality barricaded away. The things we didn't talk about, him never asking about my drinking and drugging though he had to know. I showed up at his house all the time with only a couple hours' sleep, the sleaze of the night before smeared all over me.

I remember one Yuletide disaster, in which I was Christmas shopping on Christmas Eve. With Jordan. A marine. The day turning into a shroom bender in the upper Haight, drinking Bloody Marys at the Trophy Room. Rock and roll songs on the jukebox. The Reverend Horton Heat screaming at us. Like a drill sergeant. Challenging us and we couldn't let him down. This was what happened when your heroes were train wrecks. You raced to board that same train and steer it into a tree.

Tequila shots? Sure.

You don't steer trains, stupid.

Jordan's voice getting louder. The shrooms getting louder. Me disappearing inside myself. Shouldn't someone buy a god damn Christmas gift?

There were tourists at the Trophy Room. From Australia. They explained Boxing Day and I didn't dig their accents. That was the Reverend Horton Heat and they should have stopped interrupting him.

A bourbon now? Sure.

I had to be at my dad and step-mom's house at seven a.m. the next morning. Over in the East Bay. I had young sisters who wanted to get the whole presents thing underway as soon as possible.

The ice in my Bloody Mary tasted like blood. Was that true? Shit, my tongue was bleeding. Bleeding because I bit it. Blame the Australians. Blame Boxing Day.

Chilled vodka shot? Sure.

Sisters didn't want to hear any excuses about a present-dearth, especially if it was shrooms. I said something to Jordan about buying gifts—*we should be buying them now!*—and he laughed. Marines weren't known for their emotions. And the bartender said if I played that record again he was cutting me off. If every hero of mine was a wreck themselves, well, what did you expect of me? Emulate a lifestyle until it had you by the throat. I couldn't imagine walking in my dad's house, seeing him and my step-mom and sisters without presents. What would their faces look like? God damn Australians had an extra twenty-four hours to shop. I'd changed my mind about them.

So should we do a Fernet? Yup.

My tongue healing quickly. The lights in the bar flipping on.

Me squinting and shielding my eyes. Unfit to feel such illumination. Had to get out of there. And soon we were coming down at my apartment. The shrooms getting softer. But Jordan staying too shrill.

I couldn't bear hearing him utter another syllable so I called 911. Dialing it and saying, "You have to get him out of here," and they said, "Who?" and I hung up, and half an hour later two cops at the door asking if everything was okay. Which it was not. Jordan still yapping. Me, eighteen inches tall. With a swollen tongue and disappointed sisters. The cops didn't want any part of this once they realized there was no real danger, telling me to stay put for the night and don't call them again.

Jordan going bananas once they bolted: "You called them on me?"

"I did."

"I'm leaving."

"Good."

"You're an asshole."

"Yes."

And there were things much worse than a bitten tongue. Such as a sucker punch in the gut. Such as a marine sucker-punching you. Crumpling to the floor. Hunting every inch of my lungs for something to survive on but coming up with nothing. Emitting this wheeze and the shrooms weren't helping and the sisters weren't helping and Boxing Day was salt in a wound and Jordan storming out the front door and days later, years later, my lungs finally functioning again.

Breathe in, breathe out.

Surveying the scene.

Still on floor.

Tongue still swollen.

But laughing for some reason. I was alone in my room, and it was Christmas Eve. No. Not anymore. After midnight. It was Christmas morning. Without gifts. Panic. Ran around wrapping up things found in my apartment. Olive oil. A bottle of wine. A Black Sabbath shirt that had obviously been worn.

When I arrived half an hour late, no one said anything. That was our deal. I showed up cooked out of my head and they never called me on it. Maybe that was the real gift they gave me. Or it was the worst thing.

Standing by a fake tree, faking gifts, faking feelings. Hell, even the fire was fake. The TV tuned to a station playing fire. A log on fire on the screen. A phony fireplace. Phony flames. Phony friendly Yuletide tunes tumbling from the box.

In lieu of heat. In lieu of actually buying wood and striking matches. In lieu of risking injury, singed fingers or smoke in eyes, watering and bloodshot and seeing much less than 20/20.

In lieu of something called family.

I had a headache and was sweaty and clammy, still pulsing with mushroom dust driving in my veins. I sat by the fake fire and the sisters, Jessie and Katy, ten and four respectively, kept saying things like, "Josh, what do you think this one is?" while pointing to or shaking a particular gift, and I saw how excited they were to open presents from me, their dented prince, their absentee playmate having too much fun in San Francisco to travel home, even though they only lived twenty miles away. Even though I loved them. Even though I resented their happiness. Even though love and resentment didn't dilute.

I loved my sisters more than anything, but they were a flesh and blood reminder of the fact my dad didn't want to be around me when I was their age. He didn't love me enough. Or he didn't love me like he loved them. They were who he picked to live in his stable household. Keep in mind, we weren't aware of his cancer yet. My sisters' childhoods would get turned upside down, but not on this Christmas morning.

So there I sat with the mushrooms making this unbearable. Sitting there and seeing all those smiles coming from the step-mom and sisters and even from the father. I needed to get away from their happiness. Needed to get back to where I was comfortable, with sucker punches and angry marines.

"What is this?" my four-year-old sister, Katy, said. She shook the gift I brought her back and forth.

Me shrugging my shoulders.

"Can I open this one from Josh first?" asked Katy.

My parents saying okay. Her tearing through the wrapping paper. Which was really just newspaper. Me cringing. Her pulling out that faded Black Sabbath shirt. Her holding it up. Her smiling at me. The other sister, Jess, smiling too. My parents frowning. Me avoiding any eye contact. Feeling a fever of guilt. Because she loved the shirt. Loved it! Because it was from me.

I could have given her a blanket sullied with smallpox.

Katy draped herself in the shirt's ill-fitting form and waddled over to me, the black thing hanging past her knees and she hugged me and she said, "Thanks!" and I said, "Okay," and she said, "This is perfect!" and I said, "Okay," and my sister still smiling and my parents still frowning, and my heart blackening in a real fire.

This would take all day, opening gifts and bonding and chewing chalky turkey and hucking a Frisbee and yet it would end the same way. It would end back in the Mission District. In a dive bar. Plans already hatched to roll. Snorting lines of E then popping pills too. For good measure. Better safe than sober.

And yet there were hours to endure still. Hours of happiness. Hours of resentment. Whole logs of time to burn. Feeling every bit of warmth emanating from a televised blaze.

———

I never wanted *fake* blazes. Not my style. I wanted a life wild with fires.

One time, liquored up at the Dovre Club on Valencia, I smoked out front of the bar and it was right after a different

Christmas and people had placed their dried trees on the sidewalk, and I didn't see dried Christmas trees, no way, I saw the greatest and saddest fireworks show the Mission District had ever known. So I dragged two trees into the middle of the street and torched them both. Stood close to these fires and felt their heat and yet it wasn't enough.

There were plenty more dried trees on this block and plenty on the next and so on. I could go as far as I wanted and there would always be more things to burn. Could keep hauling trees and lighting them and running farther down the block and I could look back at all these fires and flutter with a flushed happiness because I did it all.

This was all because of me.

———

But we were talking about my wedding day with Blue, and here's what I remember: An hour or so before the ceremony, helping my father get dressed. We were alone, the two of us putting on rented tuxedos, and his hands shook so badly from the chemo, the radiation, the steroids, all the terrible experimental treatments he put his body through so he could watch my sisters grow up.

He wanted to live long enough, he told me, to know them as adults. "Like you," he said. "Like how I know you."

He stood in the dressing room with his shirt unbuttoned, so frustrated with his shaking hands and too stubborn to ask for help. I said, "Let me," and started with his bottom button and worked my way to his thin throat, and he said, "Sorry," and I said, "Don't be," and he said, "It's embarrassing," and I said, "It's only us," and he said, "I love you," and I said, "I love you too," and he said, "Proud of you."

He meant it, of course. He was my father and he loved me, and I was his son and I loved him. I watched those stupid shaking hands of his as he said that he felt proud—proud of me?—why and how and what for, and I hate that during the ceremony I stood in front of him, pledging that I'd do my best to make that marriage work, for better and worse. Because I didn't. I couldn't. I lied to him, to Blue, to every witness.

Yet there were a few seconds before the wedding, before my lies. A few minutes, a pure and shining and sincere moment between father and son. I'll always have that image of his frail frame barely filling out a rented tuxedo. Not a hair left on his head. A complexion like a raw prawn.

There we were. Father and son. Me buttoning his shirt. Him speaking those three words.

———

My dad died and I had this stampeding grief, and it wanted to travel, wanted to gallop and guzzle trouble. It wanted to race off so I could waterboard my feelings with booze.

Driving on acid is underrated. Not as dangerous as you're thinking. You float down the road. Granted, it's hard not to speed. And staying in your lane is almost impossible. It's a cross between a luge and a magic carpet ride.

Okay, it's probably as dangerous as you're thinking.

I scored some acid with three of my dirtbag friends, and we drove off. Okay, I drove to Reno. On acid. They drank beers and sang along to the radio. We had it on a god awful station that played things like Kenny Loggins' "Footloose" and that became our anthem for the trip.

Downtown Reno was a super sad stash of diners, casinos, strip clubs, and cowboy bars. Nobody had any fun there. The strippers practically used nicotine patches for pasties.

Our first night was your typical hard drinking/hard drugging/take-no-prisoners bender. It's what we expected the whole weekend to be like, but Anthony got arrested early the next morning. I've never been exactly clear—and I don't think he is either—as to what he was picked up for. One theory was that he was sleeping in the hallway of a motel we weren't staying at. They frown on such behavior.

So we were killing time the next morning—Jabiz, Ben, and me—waiting for Anthony to be freed from the tank. It was before noon, say ten a.m. or thereabouts, and we were at a strip club that had a "renowned" buffet so we figured we could kill two birds with one bad idea: see naked ladies and eat at the same time.

It didn't seem to bother Jabiz or Ben, chewing their food while smiling at these working women, waiting to pounce. But I couldn't do it: The acid gave me a weird vein of morality, making it tasteless to eat food in front of the girls. I actually sat in the back of the club with my back to the stage, chewing my food like a good little boy, then joining my friends once I could ogle without worrying if I had prime rib in my teeth.

At a certain point while getting a lap dance, I asked a stripper, "Can you help us get some blow?"

"Sure."

"Here?"

"No," she said, "after my shift."

"When's that?"

"Two hours. I can't leave with a customer or I'll get fired. I'll pick you up around the corner."

I reported the good news to Jabiz and Ben. This was the thing to turn the day around. I mean, don't get me wrong, the buffet was topnotch, but some ya-yo would make sure we made it through the entire weekend with drinks in our hands.

"We should see if the DJ can play 'Footloose' while the next woman strips," I said.

Both Ben and Jabiz thought that was a stellar idea.

Unfortunately, the DJ didn't have the track. Instead, as a Kenny Loggins' consolation, he offered "Danger Zone" from the *Top Gun* soundtrack. You should have seen this woman dance to "Danger Zone." It was a wonderful sight.

———

Jabiz, Ben, and I killed the next two hours with watered-down drinks. Then the stripper—I can't remember her name so let's call her Quinn—said I should meet her in ten minutes up the block.

She drove me to one of those prefab complexes out on the edge of town. All the condos washed in beige stucco, front yards just tan gravel. We walked into her house and she vanished into the bedroom, told me to grab a beer and sit in the living room. I heard voices in the back and for the first time I got scared. I didn't know her. I could very easily get robbed. Not that their take would be worth the effort. But still, no one wants to get rolled in Reno.

Soon, she returned carrying a baby. A little boy with bright red hair. The same shade that I had as a youngster.

"This is Bobby," she said.

"Who were you talking to?"

She motioned to the baby.

"Where's the sitter?" I said.

"Anyway, you watch him for a few minutes and I'll go get the blow," Quinn said, handing him over before I had the chance to say anything back. Then she disappeared into the backyard, through the sliding glass door.

It was Bobby and me. We stared at each other. I bounced him on my knee and said, "I'm a friend of your mom's."

I held that little boy and thought about all the strange men my mom had left me with over the years, once my dad bolted for California. There was this one crazy cat, Jim B. I don't know much about him, really. He was the handyman at the company where my mom was the secretary. He had a hair trigger. I saw him wing his coffee cup at a car because the guy cut him off in traffic.

One day in his truck he chomped a cigar and said to me, "You tough?"

I was about ten years old. "Yeah, I'm tough."

"Let's see about that." He told me to place my forearm down on the armrest between us. He placed his forearm right next to mine so they touched. Then he took his lit cigar and laid it down on us, so it was burning both our arms.

"First one to move is soft as a baby's ass," said Jim.

Without any dad around I wanted to impress Jim. I wanted him to say, "Holy shit, kid, you're chiseled out of rock." But I wasn't tough. I was a ten-year-old faking it. I held my arm there, smelling the burn of his arm hair, our skin, I tried to be as tough as possible but pretty soon I jerked my arm away and rubbed the spot where the cherry kissed it.

"Toughest in all the land," Jim said, retrieving his cigar and taking some celebratory puffs.

I bet my mom had no idea about the day Jim burned my arm. I probably didn't mention it to her. Truth was I liked spending time with Jim, even if he scared me. He was a man, a tough man, and no matter how dumb it sounds now, I enjoyed being around him. Yes, he was dangerous but he gave me lots of attention. And if you spend enough time being ignored, a burning cigar on your skin isn't so bad.

"Your mom loves you," I said to Bobby, bouncing him some more. "So does your dad. They are trying their best."

Because of my sisters, I was good with babies. But Quinn didn't know that. She didn't care, needed her cut of the money from selling me an eight ball. She wasn't getting rich working the morning shift at the club.

I don't want to say apathy. Don't want to say malice. Don't want to believe Bobby was left with men like me often. Men looking to score drugs. Score anything Quinn was willing to hock. I don't want to ponder all the Jims that might have sat on this same sofa, whipping out their burning cigars or worse. I don't want to say any of that because Bobby deserves better.

———

Quinn was back in about twenty minutes, offered me a ride to town and I said I'd rather walk.

"It's eight miles," she said.

"I'll call a taxi."

"They don't come here."

"Why?"

"Just let me drive you," she said.

"Can Bobby come?"

"Of course," Quinn said. "I can't leave him here by himself, right?"

She smirked at me, and I pretended that I didn't know what her face meant. The image of Bobby left there, alone, scared and crying, clammy with a dirty diaper, while Quinn worked her morning shift at the club made me want to impale my heart, let its juice drip down and coagulate on the floor—what was the point in even having a heart when babies needed help and we wouldn't ease their suffering?

It wasn't my fault, per se, but I was there.

"Want a bump for the road?" Quinn said. It was a wretched suggestion, but I couldn't say no.

Bobby played on his blanket while we sniffed brutal eight-inch lines—lines so long you needed a running start to pack in all that powder.

The car ride back to town was quiet, Quinn and I not talking much, Bobby gurgling in the backseat. That red hair of his—of ours—I stared at it in the rearview, knowing that in a couple minutes I'd never see the boy again. He'd live his life and I'd live mine but in this wicked world our paths would never converge.

Sometimes, toward a movie's conclusion a couple quick sentences hit the screen telling the audience where this man or woman ended up down the line. And I'd like to do the same thing for Bobby. I'd like to cook up a future for him.

First, his mom gets clean.

Second, they get out of Reno.

Third, she falls in love with a good man and Bobby has a father figure. Someone who's never even smoked a cigar.

Fourth, this father raises Bobby as his own, teaching him to be kind, to be a hard worker, to honor his commitments, and this father never dies. This father lives forever.

Fifth, I want Bobby to never even try booze and drugs, swear them off just because he knows the havoc they wreaked in his mom's life before she got sober.

Sixth, Bobby is safe and solid. He is a safe and solid man with a safe and solid life.

That's what I want so badly for that innocent boy. And who knows? Maybe that's what happened.

All I can tell you for sure is that they drove off. I was alone in the motel parking lot with the blow and my dad's ghost. Anthony was probably out of jail by then. Jabiz and Ben were antsy to get high. Bobby was gone, leaving all us Jims in the rearview.

———

My childhood wasn't always lacquered in some monochrome gloom. You need to know that. We had good times, too, my mom and me. She was an amazing pianist, but because she had rheumatoid arthritis in her wrists, it hurt her to play. She drank and drugged in part so she could fight through the pain and play piano. There were other reasons she partied, but don't worry about those right now.

Just worry about the boy under her piano bench.

There he is, lying on his stomach, beneath her, listening to her play. He presses one of the piano's pedals. His mom knows what he's doing, of course. This is a game they play. She strikes some tune and pretends that she has no idea that he's hiding beneath her bench and he sends a hand out, mashing one pedal down, making each note ring on and on, and she asks, "Why does my music sound like that?" and the boy muffles a laugh, moving his hand from one pedal to another and pressing that one now, and the mother says, "I don't understand what's happening!" and the boy can barely stand it, maybe a chuckle slips out, and he sends his hand to his favorite pedal, the one that severs each note she plays, making the song sound so staccato, and he is beside himself, anticipating what will happen next, and before he knows it the music stops, the mother slowly sliding the bench back a bit and peering down at him and saying, "What are you doing down there, silly?" and he says, "Gotcha!" and she says, "Gotcha back!" and tickles him, first on the ribs, then the armpits, then cracking up herself and saying, "Will you please let me practice?" and the boy saying, "Okay," and she says, "I'm serious this time," and he says, "Okay," already smiling, and so she slides her piano bench back into position and picks the tune up where she left off and ten, twenty seconds later—however long the excited boy can endure waiting—he sends his hand out and presses the first pedal again and their routine starts over and they are so happy.

4

OF COURSE, YOU CAN ONLY RELAPSE IF YOU'VE gotten clean, and you can only get clean if there are things you promise yourself that you're never going to do, and you saw each of these promises in half like magicians' assistants, this litany of lines you will never cross, coded beliefs that are sanctified and unimpeachable, maybe a moral compass that will always point in the other direction from certain degradations, certain bad ideas, but you trample these demarcations, sprint over them like they're finish lines.

And they are, in a matter of speaking.

———

After the Peek-a-Boo Factory fiasco, I can't tell what's *true*. Meaning am I being honest about how devastated I am after seeing Ava fall, or am I hunting for a reason to relapse? Am I manufacturing motive? She wasn't even hurt, so why am I making it sound so grave?

If I zero in on my life, if I scour and skewer and stew on any aspect, I'll always locate some benign reason to give up. To fail and flee. So the question becomes, is that what I want? Do I want to end up alone and alcoholic?

No, of course not.

Yes, of course.

———

There's this secret thing about relapse: You want there to be a reason. You crave cause and effect. You want some tragedy, a trigger, something that directly leads you to a bar or a dealer's house or a corner. You want it to be easily explainable to people after the fact. You want them to hear your reason and you want them to pity you. Yes, pity! You want this captive audience to hear your ordeal and think to themselves, wow, in a similar circumstance, I would have behaved the same way.

If you have that, if they gift you that, then maybe there's a small chance you can stomach living because I'll tell you what, the shame—the electric shame—that accompanies a relapse is something to behold.

———

I had thirteen months clean the first time I relapsed. Thirteen months, gone, given away on a day bulging with ordinariness. No glorious incident, no lethal news, no reason…

This was before Ava, before Lelo and I were married. We lived in the Mission District, at the corner of 20th and Valencia. Coincidentally, we were right across the street from where I used to live with Blue, but I tried not to take that as a sign for a lack of progress. Signs, I rationalized, weren't that on-the-nose.

It had been a normal morning, Lelo and I showering and swigging coffee and going to work. A morning with meetings, emails, a morning that can't be separated from any of a hundred just like it. Conjoined mornings. All anonymous and bland.

A morning with a bagel and carrot juice, where my boss was distracted and so I wrote at my desk. I was pretty deep into my third novel, *Damascus*, and one of the reasons I tolerated this shitty start-up job was that I had huge chunks of unsupervised time. My boss was a failed musician and he dug that I wrote books. He knew I scribbled on the clock and maybe it made him feel like a patron of the arts. I have no idea what that sad cat was all about, but he's a part of this story. In a couple hours, he'll invite me to lunch. I'll go. He'll order a scotch. So will I.

I won't mention rehab, won't utter one peep about trying to be a better person.

It was 2010; it was a Monday or Thursday or Friday; it was winter or spring or summer; I was content or feeling stifled; it was another reconstituted morning until I ruined everything.

———

Was boredom a part of my relapse?

I don't remember consciously thinking about this then, but as I look back, I wonder if I was simply bored, learning to live quietly. Before rehab, I had a life flush with chaos, and now there was routine, carrot juice and conjoined mornings and whatnot, and perhaps this inflamed some tacit impatience, some ammunition I didn't know was live until it was too late.

Maybe I didn't want to ruin everything that day; maybe I just needed a splash of anarchy.

———

The other thing about that job was when I first got the gig, they issued an email account with a temporary password, *Changeme!*

But I never did.

How could I?

Thirteen months sober felt like a long time to me. So when that sad start-up boss, Neal, invited me out for lunch, I saw no reason to say no. Why couldn't I go out and nurse a soda water while Neal drank his lunch? He was notorious around the office for getting loaded over a midday snack. First thing in the morning, he lurched toward his desk, head down, all tousled and dejected, that slow chain-gang shuffle, knowing he'd spend his day slamming rocks with his sledgehammer and belting out spirituals. But his whole demeanor was different when he returned to the office from lunch, after throwing back a bunch of cocktails. He was giddy, smiling and peppy, like a kid at Disneyland taking his picture with Goofy.

I didn't know this at the time, but my thirteen months off booze and drugs didn't mean shit if I was too afraid to tell people I was sober. I hated saying that, admitting it.

Why?

Well, I'd always hated sober people. I spent my twenties tending bar and sober people were the enemy. I spent my twenties and early thirties as a drunk and an addict and sober people were the enemy on that front too. They were teetotaling cowards. They were scared to live recklessly. They were cautious and safe and timid, all things I never wanted to be.

So during that first thirteen months of my sobriety, I never told anyone I was clean. Nobody except my dearest friends, say five or six heads. I harbored that detail like a diagnosis.

"Dewar's and a beer back," Neal said to the bartender, a few blocks from our office.

"That sounds good," I said, knowing that ordering a drink didn't mean I had to put the liquid in my mouth. I didn't have to swallow. There was nothing that said I had to gulp the whole shot down.

"I'll join you guys," said the bartender. He poured us three huge shots of scotch, triples. That was one nice thing about drinking during the day with a thirsty bartender: He wanted playmates, so his generosity knew no bounds.

They snatched theirs and looked at me; I grabbed mine and stared back.

Soon, all three of us held our scotches in the air.

Soon, all three of us drank them.

———

The other thing no one tells you about relapse is that you think you can drink as much as you could before you quit. I was out of practice but I didn't care. Tossing back scotches round for round with Neal.

We laughed and told war stories and lied and thumped our chests and our bravado blew up like helium balloons floating over our heads.

And for a couple hours, this was fun. I was having fun. Drunk enough that I didn't care what I was dismantling. I was hours away from that.

But I did think about Kae. That's something I clearly remember. I went to take a leak and after washing my hands, I thrust them under the automatic hand dryer. Feeling that warm breath, thinking about his donut shop essay, the life he gave away being busted back. I swear the whole bathroom smelled like car exhaust. Fumes filling my lungs with polluted beauty.

For a few seconds, Kae was with me.

———

And at a certain point I blacked out. Last thing I remember was Neal and me doing another scotch and the bartender telling me to stop yelling. He had no idea who he was dealing with. I never stopped.

Never in a million years did I want to sober up. This was how I wanted to feel forever. So cooked I couldn't stand, couldn't do much of anything, except drink and sit and yell, drink and sit and yell. This was a perfect way to spend your life.

And then I was being zipped in a body bag, the whole world disappearing.

Freebies were dreams, our brains vacationing in squalor. Going back to old lifestyles. Popping bottles or pills or plunging needles into veins or muscles. But these freebies only happened in our imaginations. Freebies, also known as harmless little films flickering of relapse.

One counselor in rehab told me to enjoy these inebriated fantasies. "Like a sex dream," she said. "Fun with no consequences."

So for a shot glass full of seconds, I thought that whole afternoon session with Neal was fake, a fever dream for my subconscious, some imaginary debacle and I would wake up refreshed. Freaked out but refreshed.

Coming to the next morning one thing was obvious: My nose was broken.

A couple other immediately obvious things, I was at my apartment but had no recollection of getting there. I wore only underwear, which meant someone must have helped me out of my clothes. The other obvious thing was that I was alone in the bedroom. That was when this popped in my sick head: *did I get caught?* Because if Lelo didn't know, maybe I could lie about it. For a drunk, that whole thing about a tree falling in the forest—and did it make a sound if no one heard?—it worked for relapse too. Meaning I might not have made a sound when I fell. And if the only people who knew I'd gone on a quick run were Neal and the bartender, I could live with that. Just never go back to that job, that bar. Just pretend that yesterday never happened.

"Are you okay?"

I hoped that was my broken nose talking, but it sounded like Lelo.

"I've never seen someone get so sick," she said.

"What happened?"

She told me I came home early last night, about seven. My face had dried blood all over it. I got sick right away and every half an hour after. She thought about taking me to the emergency room, but I talked her out of it between retches.

"Yeah, but what happened?" I said.

"You tell me, Josh."

"I've ruined it…"

"I'll go get you a Gatorade."

"Thanks for taking care of me," I said.

She looked at me with what I assumed was mauling disappointment. She was sad, tired. She'd been up all night doting on a useless drunkard. What really ripped my heart out was how I'd tricked her, teasing her with these thirteen months, a year and change of something better, and then one day our clean life was gone. And for no reason. I didn't like scotch, I didn't like Neal, I didn't like drinking in some snooty tapas joint, I didn't like my mysterious broken nose. There was nothing I could blame this on except myself, my Sirens.

How was Lelo supposed to forgive me and why should she? And how should she ever believe me after? If I'd relapsed once, why wouldn't it happen again and again and again?

Lelo had been my girl four years when I finally went to rehab. She'd seen the caveman, seen a lot of the stupidity first hand. "Thanks for the Gatorade," I said. "That's nice of you."

She left our apartment and I could hear her heels clacking down the front stairs, could hear the huge weighted front door of our apartment building slam behind her. "Please come back," I whispered.

The clock said it was 7:41 in the morning. I staggered to the bathroom and threw up. Flushed the toilet and crashed on the bathroom floor. There were streaks of vomit everywhere. No wonder the muscles in my sides ached. I must have gotten sick thirty times.

I lay down. Why go back to bed only to be summoned here to dry heave? I threw myself into the tub and cranked up the cold. It dribbled from our hopeless showerhead.

Thirteen months, busted just like my nose.

Lelo was leaving me. She had to. I'd made it impossible for her to stay. That Gatorade was a parting gift, a concession. I drove her away, like I did with Blue.

———

"Either you go to rehab or move out," said Blue. This was in July 2005, four years before I tried getting sober for the first time. It was the morning of my birthday. It might sound malicious on Blue's part to threaten me like this on my birthday, and it probably was, but in her defense, I deserved it, staying out the whole night before and not calling, crawling in about eight a.m. with a coke nosebleed.

"I'm sorry," I said.

"I care less and less with every apology," she said. Then she went to work, telling me we'd talk more about it when she got home. She was disgusted, and I couldn't blame her, and it made me nostalgic for the days when she dug bedlam. And she used to be a card-carrying nutcase. Like the night we went to see Beckett's *Waiting for Godot*. I bought us kickass seats, way up front, and we decided to dress in our best Beckettian costumes. All black, of course. Eyeliner smeared in great ovals around our eyes. Hair teased up and pasted in weird gravity-defying geometries.

And we cocktailed starting three hours before the show and even shared a bottle of champagne in the car on our way to the theater. For most heads, drinking and driving was a two-step process but not in my life: I loved to drink while driving. Something I used to do all the time and even sometimes now I get the itch behind the wheel, reaching for a bottle like an amputee scratching a phantom limb.

Anyway, on this night we imbibed a bit too much, and Blue was asleep in her seat midway through the first act. That would have probably been fine if she didn't start snoring. Really snoring. Beckett himself would have *loved* this, a beautiful woman conked out at his show and cranking up her snore like it was running through Marshall stacks. But the people around us did not dig Blue's music, and I shook her a few times, saying, "You okay?" and she said, "I want to go home," and I said, "Really?" and she said, "Will you carry me?"

Will I carry her? Of course, I'll carry her.

I swooped Blue up in my arms and kicked my way to the aisle, trudging away from the actors, the audience, feeling proud of her, the scene she was making. It was a perfect night.

But it wasn't, I guess. Eventually, she wanted to stay awake, see the show. Our lifestyle wore on her until she quit the restaurant biz to be an acupuncture assistant. Blue binged still but only on tinctures, tilting cocktails of herbal extracts and water. We had a huge shelf in our kitchen that was dedicated to all her murky herbs.

The drunker my lifestyle became, hers swirled with healing beverages. No more coffee in the morning but a shot of Siberian ginseng. No pills to sleep but valerian root.

Sometimes when home alone, I'd cut lines of blow or heroin out on her special herbal section, thinking I was proving a point, but what would that even prove? That I was petty?

Blue was evolving into something new and vibrant and better, and I stayed one species behind.

Even if I knew she was right on my birthday, I wasn't going to rehab. I was under the influence of something else: being *obstinate*. Every junkie knows it well, all our friends telling us to get some help, get our shit together, but hell no, we're holding out. This ain't closing time, Jack. This ain't the bottom. This life can get much worse and we'll show you, thank you very much.

So once Blue left for the acupuncture clinic that morning, I packed my favorite clothes, which were all dirty, fishing them from the hamper and filling a yellow duffel bag and bolting. Went straight to the dive bars on 16th street, hell bent on celebrating my birthday with or without Blue.

Years later, she told me she didn't think we were splitting up for good that day—thought we were only having a fight, that yes, she issued an ultimatum but it was only to scare me, to get me to come to my senses and sober up so we could be right.

She said, "I cracked the door and you ran through it."

That was the end of our three-year marriage.

Being a drunk demands that of you: vanishing from all kinds of required life.

———

I plopped my yellow duffel bag down on the stool next to me, like a drinking buddy. Let's call her Josephine because I needed some female companionship, even if she was chockfull of stinky argyle socks and plaid pants.

She and I had picked the Kilowatt for our first stop because it was easy to get drugs there in the afternoon. Any bar would have access to narcotics once the sun dipped down, but at the Kilowatt, you could see people from noon on with cocaine running around the rims of their noses like salt on margarita glasses.

Since this was a birthday bash, Josephine and I decided to get an eight ball. Spare no expense! We needed an ample supply of party favors to do the job right.

The Kilowatt was a narrow room, a weird maze of tables and booths with spilled liquor smeared all over their tops. Rock and roll always piped, and dogs scurried between tables, looking for handouts.

Really, we were all looking for handouts at the Kilowatt.

On that day, the bar was all men—a bunch of testosterone pouches hunched over one spirit or another, in various stages of spoil. We could have been lined up for a time lapse educational video on the ruin of alcoholism. There was a young, skinny, speedy punk sitting at the bar, tapping both his feet and talking mach syllables, his Mohawk pasted to such jagged tips it could have been a throwing star, and there was me, around thirty, still handsome but carrying that doughy drunkard's weight in his face and neck, and at a table was a couple fortyish fellas reeking of alimony, botched rehabs, kids not bothering to text dear old dad on his birthday, and finally our crown jewel, our destiny, a raving broken pathos machine, somewhere in his sixties, nose a mosaic of fissured veins.

Josephine and I didn't want to be around them anymore so we had a couple shots, a couple beers, and decided to troll. Went to Delirium next, the joint with my favorite sign in the city—the one behind the bar that said *Service for the Sick*—and again, not much in the department of the fairer sex, so Josephine and I made our way to Zeitgeist, sitting at a picnic table out back on the patio with a pitcher of wheat beer, sneaking bumps of coke off my (former) apartment key when no one was looking.

There were groups of other people like me—tattooed hipsters, artists—congregated at other picnic tables. Social D played. I was the only one alone, the only one snuggling up to a duffel bag. I needed to fix that and fast.

"Listen," I said to Josephine, "I like you, but I need to find an actual person to hang out with today."

My friends, all growing increasingly absent when I went on a binge, even Shany, had plans when I called and told them that Blue kicked me out on my birthday and I needed their assistance to bender properly.

They knew what was coming and excuses sprouted like a rash.
Root canals.

Tax audits.

Vasectomies.

Boob jobs.

Anything so they didn't have to meet me and watch what they knew was going to happen. I brought the duffel bag closer to my mouth. "The plan," I said to her, "is to find somebody to go to dinner with me tonight. I want to keep that reservation."

Earlier in the week, Blue and I had made plans to go to a fancy seafood restaurant. I was going to go there that night and eat overpriced fish and drink overpriced champagne and I was going to blow out the candle stuck in an overpriced dessert and I was going to have a great fucking birthday.

"Where should we go next?" I said to Josephine.

———

Her name was Sadie. I met her at… well, I don't actually remember where I met her. Maybe Benders. Maybe the 500 Club or Doc's Clock or Mission Bar or The Attic. Could be the Lone Palm. Josephine and I were thorough explorers that day. All I know is that I saw the lovely Sadie sitting at a bar by herself. She was black Irish, and I was a sucker for that mix of dark hair and blue eyes. She sipped whiskey on the rocks by herself.

I slid Josephine under my barstool and sat a couple down from Sadie.

I knew how to seduce her because I'd done this many times. I wouldn't talk to her directly at first, chatting with the bartender so Sadie could hear. I'd be funny, charming, and when Sadie finally initiated eye contact—like our interaction was her idea— I'd offer to buy her a drink, and anybody nipping whiskey by herself in the late afternoon would accept, and that was exactly what happened.

"It's my birthday," I said.

"Bullshit," she said, "that's just a line."

"I wouldn't lie to you."

"Show me your ID."

I did. She spent thirty seconds analyzing the information.

"Should you really be an organ donor?" Sadie asked.

"I'm in tip-top shape."

"You're old, too."

"I'm twenty-nine."

"That's old."

"Would you like a bump?"

Pretty soon, we huddled in the little girls' room, in a stall, and I cut a couple rips on the back of the toilet, handing her a rolled up dollar and saying, "Ladies first."

"Prince Charming, huh?"

———

I waited until we were good and loaded and told Sadie the truth: Blue kicked me out, and I had a dinner reservation that I wanted to keep. "No strings attached," I said. "Come to dinner with me. Let's drink champagne and then you go your way and I'll go mine."

"Don't you want to take someone who actually knows you?"

How could I tell her that people who knew me hated me? How could I tell her that she was my only chance? "That's the last thing I want," I said to Sadie.

"Why?"

"Are you hungry or not?"

"Of course I'm not hungry," she said, "and neither are you. We did a gram of blow. But I'll come to your weird birthday party."

———

We walked in the restaurant and I told the hostess my last name. She didn't know my wife threw me out. Didn't know that my dirty laundry was crammed in the yellow duffel bag over my shoulder. All she knew was that a bleary eyed guy showed up in the company of a gorgeous young woman, and there was nothing wrong with that.

I ordered a $75 appetizer, a tower of shellfish and oysters and Dungeness crab and lobster. Of course, I couldn't stop blowing lines, so each expensive bite tasted terribly—a cocktail of saltwater brine and cocaine drip—but that wasn't going to stop me. I choked down every gluttonous forkful.

Sadie sat across from me swigging champagne and shaking her head. "I've seen drunks do oddball shit," she said, watching me cracking meat from a crab claw, "but you are your own animal."

"I'm not my own enemy."

"I said animal."

I accidentally kicked Josephine under the table. "Oh."

"And you can't argue with that, can you?" she said. "Aren't you an animal?"

These weren't the things I wanted to be talking about. This was a birthday party, and I was the guest of honor. Sadie called me an animal, so I meowed—the nerdiest, girliest meow I could muster, channeling my inner eight-year-old and getting a good one right in Sadie's face.

Meow!

We laughed. We made a toast: *to kitties the world over.* We kissed. And for a moment, it worked. I completely forgot who I was.

"I want you to fuck me," said Sadie.

"I'd like that."

"Now," she said. "I want you to fuck me now."

We moved toward the back where the restaurant had two unisex bathrooms. Both were locked, but we were the only ones in line so we kissed. A woman walked out of one of them, startled by how we were going at it, but we couldn't care about that.

Once the door was locked, Sadie ripped off her jeans and panties and hopped on the sink, balancing herself, holding up her shirt to play with her nipples. I still stood by the door and pulled my cock out, and I stared in between Sadie's spread legs, her pubic hair cut to a buzz, and I licked my lips, salivating, slowly moved toward her, only two more strides and I'd be there, with her, I'd be there with her and I'd be far away from all my mistakes and far away from my conscience and far away from anything or anyone who could judge me, two strides and I'd fall to my knees and taste her.

But I never made it.

I couldn't make it.

I couldn't make it because everything changed.

One minute she sat on the sink with her pretty pale legs spread wide, and the next minute the sink ripped from the wall, water spraying everywhere, Sadie landing amidst the shattered porcelain.

We looked at each other, and Sadie laughed like crazy, lying on the ground. It was a small miracle that she didn't cut up her ass, but thankfully she was fine. I put my dick away and helped her up, knew that the sink had made a crazy loud noise and soon workers from the restaurant would be there wanting to know what had happened, what had I done now, what was the latest thing I busted?

After giving my phone and driver's license numbers to the manager of the restaurant—"You're going to pay for the damage! You're going to pay for what you did!"—Sadie, Josephine, and I went back to the Mission District dive bars. Back home. We didn't belong in that posh place.

The cocaine had been the pre-dinner drug of choice, but now it was time to go down, getting some pills to finish the job, finish this birthday boy off. And that was what must have happened because next thing I knew I startled myself awake in the morning. I was so thirsty, having no idea where I was, whole body throbbing for some sugar.

Sadie was passed out next to me, and I snuck out of her room with Josephine. Found a bottle of beer in her kitchen, brought it into the bathroom, turned on the shower. The room filled with steam, while I stood there naked, sipping that beer.

I closed the toilet lid and set Josephine there, unzipped her to change my clothes. The waft that escaped her maw, the stench of my dirty laundry, was a sucker punch and I retched.

Then I leaned over and stuck my head right inside Josephine's guts, shaking my face around in there, burrowing as deep as I could.

I was a nude homeless drunkard hiding in a duffel bag.

———

And then years later I was a nude relapsed drunkard hiding in a cold shower. Fresh off a relapse. A mysterious broken nose. The good life, given away. Probably losing Lelo.

I made myself a promise lying in the cold running water. Promised I'd go to a meeting and tell a roomful of people what I'd done, promised I'd at least try to build on this last thirteen months; maybe there is wisdom in that old cliché, "Relapse is part of recovery."

Because though I hated myself for drinking again, at least I didn't enjoy it. I was throwing up and my nose had looked better. It could have gone the other way. I could have loved going back out. It could have been some seedy reconciliation, seeing an old flame and kissing her passionately, pledging devotion, eloping, living out our time in splendid squalor.

Maybe I was lucky that didn't happen so my relapse could stop at one day. A lot of people aren't that lucky, and they shack up with that mistress. You might think "lucky" is the wrong word here, but I'm serious: That maniac lying in the bathtub, shivering, he's fortunate.

One thing was certain: I wasn't going to keep my sobriety a secret anymore. I'd scream it in Kae's tailpipe like it was a microphone.

———

Something amazing happened once I finally peeled myself out of the shower. Lelo came back. She had that Gatorade and a breakfast bagel. She hugged me. She said, "Let's lie down together."

She and I had started dating right after Blue and I had split up back in 2005. She knew I was an alcoholic, and she was there when things went from bad to worse to suicidal. She stayed through all that nonsense and it looked like she was going to stay through my relapse, too.

I want to say something here about the nature of love—how it's hard as a diamond and can't be scratched, no matter what. But I don't believe that. Many loves end; hell, most of them do. That doesn't mean they're any less *love*. Diamonds might be hard but they can be lost. Anything, everyone, can be lost.

I loved Blue and it ended.

I love Lelo and thankfully, she's in the next room right now. It doesn't make any sense to me why she stayed. What was in it for Lelo back then?

We were out walking with Ava yesterday, and I said, "I don't understand why you didn't leave me."

"What do you mean?"

"I was liquored up all the time."

"You were a good boyfriend," she said. "Generous. You were nice and funny and charming, just like you are now."

I didn't like this answer because I feel different. I like to separate myself from that caveman as much as possible. I'm a better person. He's gone. I'm here.

"Don't make yourself the bad guy," she said.

She meant in this book. Meant don't punish myself page after page, but how can I do anything else? This book is my barrel of blame, and I'm going to guzzle the stuff.

"Just make sure and tell the truth," she said. "Tell everyone that I'm an angel."

She was joking, but I agreed with her.

I couldn't find any other answer.

I don't deserve anyone's loyalty, anyone's open heart.

So she's an angel.

Full stop.

She must be.

5

ONCE YOU'RE CLEAN, THERE ARE NO MERIT BADG-
es for being around booze. No bonus points if you stay up late,
sitting with the animals, watching them gobble pills. I had too
much confidence that day with Neal, or maybe it wasn't actual
confidence, but a masquerade: It might have just been my hiber-
nating junkie tricking me. It might have been his way of luring
me into dangerous situations, knowing eventually I'd collapse to
the occasion.

That afternoon drinking with Neal happened because of
something a few months prior, when I was fresh from rehab. I
was in treatment most of January and the beginning of February
2009, and my first novel was published that June. I had to go on
book tour without drinking, something I knew was going to be
challenging. I even mentioned it to one of the drug counselors
before leaving rehab and she said, "Listen, drugs don't care if
you're from Yale or jail, Josh. Maybe don't go on tour."

I didn't have the heart to tell her that I went to a state college.
"I have to go," I said.

"You have to stay sober."

"I will."

"Be careful."

I was nervous but was doing it anyway. Maybe that's called overconfidence, or it's the tunnel vision that happens when your greatest dream in life is coming true, and the thing I wanted more than anything was to be a published author.

I had worked relentlessly on my writing for years, though I found it accidentally. My initial creative love back in my teens and early twenties was playing music, singing and slamming out power chords on a '71 Strat, even strapped on a bass in one outfit. I dug writing songs, gigging out. But what I hated about it was I needed other people to express myself. There was always some asshole in the band who was a flake or a diva or a drunk. Granted, that asshole was me, but I was tired of the whole hive thing. I was an avid reader even then, especially when I was hungover. Those mornings, I loved sipping six-packs in bed and reading Burroughs, Selby, Céline, Acker, Plath, Braverman—anyone who abused themselves.

So after another band's breakup, I decided to write. All I needed were some stories, and I had plenty of those.

My ghostwriters were drugs. I sat down around midnight armed with booze and coke, sometimes opiates. I wrote and wrote and pretty soon the Jameson bottle dwindled and I'd blackout, but keep writing till the next morning.

Looking back now, I'm reminded of the Brothers Grimm. They told a story about a cobbler who needed help making his inventory and by some wondrous chance a couple of elves showed up in the middle of the night and built him some kick-ass shoes.

I worked the same way with alcohol and drugs, and my whiskey elves never disappointed. I mean, they didn't always write the prettiest prose—cocaine isn't known to instill poetry—but they usually unearthed interesting images, haunting motifs. It was completely sub/unconscious writing, with me having no idea what I'd done until I read the pages the next day.

Writing became an obsession and soon, I couldn't go a day without scribbling.

And apparently, I was okay at it. Flung some short stories at a couple lit mags and they got accepted right away. No money, but a little literary gasoline in my tank, cranking up my imagination and work ethic to get back at it. I fell in love with the form, the solitude. Fell in love with creating characters, worlds from scratch, bringing consciousnesses to life.

Blue was on board. We weren't married yet, but were dating seriously. She was a poet, and she wanted us to be wild writers together, wanted sensuous, filthy adventures.

"You be my Henry Miller," she'd say, "and I'll be your Anaïs Nin."

Who was I to argue with such an opulent arrangement?

I'd met her one day at a restaurant where I tended bar. Suddenly, there was this stunning brunette, a new hire, polishing silverware. She was half-Chinese, half-Irish, super skinny.

I unpacked wine boxes, and the owner sat at the bar reading the newspaper. I pointed to the brunette, "Who's that?"

"New server. Named Blue."

"You should call her 'Josh-will-have-me-in-the-sack-in-six-weeks.'"

"I'm not participating in this conversation anymore," he said. "I don't like lawsuits."

And it was a bit longer than six weeks, but Blue and I were having sex soon after. We'd drink and write and sniff E and read to each other. It was that age where you can imagine yourself changing the world with your words. That age where there was a wick of creative madness burning inside, and life was a laboratory, each day an experiment to become a better writer. Nothing was more important than splattering sentences on paper.

We were completely immersed in our art. With no other practical concerns. Before babies or mortgages or careers. Before stock options or car payments. This was when booze and drugs were there, sure, but they hadn't staged their coup.

The best example of this newfound dedication to writing was how I actually generated material. I worked with all the lights in the apartment off, the only illumination coming from my computer—the ecosystem of my book being like the moon in an empty sky.

There was nothing else alive.

In order to become the best writer I could, I decided to get an MFA. College was never my bag, but learning to be a writer felt different. I cared about my craft so much that I could be a good student, I was sure of it.

———

There was a crappy old TV show called *Quantum Leap* and every episode started with the main character, a scientist/time traveler, beamed into someone else's body and he didn't know who he was or where he was in space-time, had to figure all those things out on the fly, and that described my first night of graduate school: I was Alcoholic Quantum Leaping.

Which meant I got too drunk before school and blacked out.

Which meant I came out of it sitting in a classroom, having no idea how I got there or what I'd been saying or doing.

Ten people talking books. A professor pontificating. And blacked-out me.

Not the first impression I hoped to make.

My day had started off in an excited manner. I couldn't wait for grad school. Hanging out with other nerds who dug words the way I did.

A new friend had invited me to a baseball game that afternoon before school and I figured no sweat, catch a Giants game, then go to USF.

Simple, right?

But as we walked to our seats we passed too many beer stands for me not to get thirsty and offer to buy a round, seeing as how it was only one p.m. and school didn't start for five hours so it was no big deal, just one harmless cup of suds, and Scott was too much of a gentleman not to reciprocate a round of beers by the second inning and I was raised right and knew to meet his kindness with a skyscraping consideration of my own, buying not just beers this time but also whiskey shots and Scott didn't come of age in a wolves' den and knew about etiquette and brought the same combo back and we ping ponged rounds until we decided to ditch that dumb game and hunker down in a dive bar and I lost contact with the world.

One time, I went scuba diving in Cozumel and down there, they drift-dive: People sinking to a hundred feet in the ocean and getting swept up in the current, moving through the water without swimming at all. Floating, weightless. The boat followed your trail of bubbles, picking you up, say, forty minutes later in an entirely different spot from where you went under.

That's what blacking out is like. Submerged. Zero gravity. A specter in the world's current, slithering and gliding like seaweed. Until the minute you were pulled back in the boat, back to your life.

In the case of my first night of grad school, that happened when someone said, "What do you think, Josh?" and unfortunately that somebody happened to be the professor, and I didn't say anything back at first, looking around at the other people sitting at this table, looking at them looking at me, knowing I must have stunk like stale spirits and spongy saliva, knowing that I'd probably shot my mouth off and made a fool out of myself already and aborted this whole opportunity before it even got a chance to succeed.

I should run out of there because I couldn't do a thing right, couldn't stay sober for one god damn afternoon, couldn't take care of the things that mattered to me. I tried to stay calm, plastering on a poker face and saying to the professor, "Can you come back to me?"

"Who else wants to go?" he said.

Someone volunteered. I surveyed my surroundings. None of my classmates eyeballed me. I knew those gazes, the sideways double-takes, the periphery-sneak-a-peek when I'd made a fool of myself, tossing a garbage can at a window for no reason other than it was Cinco de Mayo, pulling my cock out in public, throwing up under a bar and ordering another drink, any of a hundred dim things that seemed to happen.

I stayed quiet the remaining hour of class. Still loaded at the end. The teacher didn't say he and I needed to talk privately; either I'd gotten away with it or it had been such a nightmare that he planned on telling his superiors and I'd be heaved from the program tomorrow.

I didn't know and I didn't care.

Or I did care.

But there was nothing to do about it.

I searched my pockets and found a gram of cocaine, slipped in the school's bathroom to blow a rip, cutting one humungous drift on the back of the toilet.

That was when I wondered how I got to school.

I probably drove. I was a serial drunk driver. But I called Scott, hoping he might tell me I did the responsible thing, hailing a cab. Unfortunately, not. Scott said I sped away from the bar, blaring The Clash.

There was nothing to do except wander the streets around campus until I found my ride.

That was the thing about Quantum Leaping: All the particulars were lost to you. You had a body, atoms and molecules and shame, but anything requiring context couldn't be grasped.

I didn't have a jacket and strolled the roads, up and down, for what felt like a hundred years, but was probably less than half an hour. Then another student who I had met at the orientation a couple weeks prior, Randy, stopped his car and asked if I needed a lift.

I got in and he smiled at me, saying, "Where to?" and I told him I couldn't remember where I'd parked and he took a closer look, a closer smell, and asked, "Are you okay?"

I did the only respectable thing: I lied.

"I'm diabetic," I said. "My sugar's not so good and I can't remember where I parked."

"Let's get you something to eat."

"No, I need to get home."

"Where's your car?"

I should have stopped talking there, but the cocaine was like a coach, coaxing me to make this lie the most convincing, surely Oscar-nominated clod that could fall from my mouth, and it clanked out of me, a whole spiel about how I'd had diabetes since elementary school and I normally was good at keeping my sugar balanced, but I'd gone to the Giants game earlier and my only options were junk food at the stadium and had to go straight to class and forgot to pack a protein-rich dinner in Tupperware and _____.

Who cared what else oozed from my lips?

Point was I'd blacked out and came to in the middle of class and my car was MIA and poor Randy had to listen to me blather until we finally found it. I smiled and pointed at my car like we'd discovered America.

"Thanks," I said, opening the door.

"Should you be driving?" Randy asked.

It was right there, in his eyes.

"I'll be fine," I said.

"I'm happy to drive you home."

"No thanks."

"Be safe," he said.

Still drunk, still coked up, still the best drunk driver in town, I made it home unscathed. Blue was zonked on the couch, watching reruns of a terrible sitcom. I tried sneaking by her to the shower, but she muted the TV and asked, "How was your first night?"

I barely said three words before she interrupted me.

"Are you loaded?" she said.

Everything came uncorked, blurting the whole day out to her and crashing in her lap, kicking and wailing.

I said, "Why can't I..."

"Why can't you what?" she said.

"Why can't I... do better?"

She didn't answer, spent her energy consoling me, letting me writhe around, letting me gnash my teeth, purge until I pulled it together enough to say, "I think I got away with it."

If sympathy and empathy could evaporate, Blue's was gone in an instant.

"What?" she said.

"The teacher didn't say anything to me after."

"You've been looking forward to writing school forever."

"I know."

"So you didn't get away with anything," she said.

"You know what I mean."

"I don't know what you mean, Josh. No one does."

She threw me out of her lap, un-muting the TV and staring at the sitcom.

She watched her show, and I lived mine, making my way to the shower, holding my head under the water, hoping that this episode of *Quantum Leap* was almost over and as the next one kicked off, I'd come to in a life unlike anything I'd ever known.

———

There were no consequences for my quantum leap. The teacher never mentioned it, nor did the other students, not even Randy. My graduate classes were every Tuesday and Wednesday nights, and I never screwed up like that again for the whole two-and-a-half-year program. In fact, I swore off going out with my peers. They all went drinking after every class, but I never tagged along, didn't trust myself.

During the summer between the first and second years of the program, I had a one-on-one thesis instruction with a professor, Karl. I had to give him roughly a hundred pages over the summer, and we'd get together a few times and talk about the material. We met in coffee shops, in the Mission or the Castro.

Karl was a fantastic reader, and I learned a lot that summer. For our last meeting, I turned in a short story called "Vulgar Transmissions from an Awful Galaxy." It was about a cocaine aficionado who worked in a restaurant, having trouble balancing his habit and being congenial to the customers. It was a solid story, the best one I'd ever written, and Karl agreed.

"I don't have any notes," he said. "This one was a gift from the muse."

It was exactly what I needed to hear. The night before had been a rough one, slugging Fernet half the night, then switching to tequila, which was always a hazardous combination. Tequila could kill you.

So being praised was a great salve, a hangover cure. It was the future I wanted so badly.

"Should I send it out to mags?" I said to Karl.

"Why not?"

My nose started bleeding. I don't remember whether it erupted right after he said that, or three minutes later, nine? But it bled and I brought my hands up to catch the drips, excused myself to the bathroom and never wanted to go back out and face him. I wanted him to know me only as an artist, one with talent. Wanted him to know me on Tuesdays and Wednesdays, not who I was the rest of the week.

Coincidentally, in my story, "Vulgar Transmissions from an Awful Galaxy," the main character kept running into the bathroom to check his nose (and of course enjoy another bump). Each new trip brought increased anxiety for him, the horror of being found out.

I was on the cusp of being discovered for my drug problem that morning with Karl. Without any guidance to help me improve my writing, I'd tend bar for thirty years, till I found out about a cirrhotic liver, my dreams pickled right along with my organs. I'd ignore the doctor's warnings to shirk booze and keep swigging spirits and eventually I'd drop dead at work, keeling down on the bar mat. The customers wouldn't even care, once they realized no one was going to stop them from filling up their own glasses.

Everything was on the house when the bartender died.

I was never able to publish "Vulgar Transmissions from an Awful Galaxy," even though I sent it to a ton of mags. Guess it wasn't a gift from the muse, after all. One common theme from editors' criticism was this: *Why should I care about some drug addict?*

Here was what I wanted to email back: *Because he's me. Because, despite all evidence to the contrary, he's trying. He just doesn't know how to stop and shouldn't that elicit some god damn empathy? What makes you such a calloused and ruthless reader?*

But I sent this instead: "Thanks for taking the time to read my work."

I split from the bathroom, so scared to see Karl. But luckily he was cool about it. Not like there was much to say, really. I wasn't going to cook up any lavish excuses like that night with Randy. I'd just tell Karl the truth if he asked. I had a cocaine nosebleed. What's the big deal?

———

My last semester in grad school was when Blue threw me out, the summer I packed my dirty laundry in Josephine. The summer of couch surfing. A plaid couch, one of corduroy. Stripes. One with cigarette burns. One so white and spotless that I couldn't get comfortable, knowing I'd leave some streak. A couch that had punk rock stickers on its armrests. There's the couch that smelled like cats, and there were the cats themselves, crawling on me all night, an intruder in their den. The cats kept me up. Sure, I felt like shit the next day. But their fur and their faces and their paws and their purrs, it was nice to be walked on like that.

I didn't so much surf these couches as I clutched them like pieces of driftwood.

I was at Matty's house. Or Rick's. Or Molly's, Mike's, Heidi's, Johnny's, Cat's, Jessica's, Nicole's, Erin's, Joge's, Sharbel's, Rob's, Tim's, Ross's. I spent a couple at Shany's. Buffy and Kevin let me spend a few nights on their thrashed couch, just so there was someone around to curb their fighting.

I had to bring Josephine to my final thesis meeting, along with the manuscript that would become my first novel, *Some Things that Meant the World to Me*. I was working with Kate that summer. She was hard on me, demanding rigorous revisions, which might seem impossible considering all the couches I clung to during that nomadic summer, might seem like I'd be too scattered, too volatile, but the opposite was true: I found sanctuary in the novel. It was the only place where I wasn't lost.

Kate sat across from me, having no idea that my whole life was in that yellow duffel bag.

"Do you think I can publish this?" I said.

"When it's ready," she said.

It was a fair, measured response, though it wasn't what I wanted. Kate, unbeknownst to her, had become my surrogate mother over the summer. Except I wasn't her child. I was a grown man with a duffel bag.

"You know what you have to do, right?" said Kate.

She meant with the book. She was asking if I understood the plan we'd put together to make improvements. She was trying to verify if I felt prepared to tackle the remix over the next few months. Kate would leave me behind and have a whole new batch of students to worry about.

"Yeah, I do," I said, "and thanks. Thanks for teaching me so much."

"I can't wait to see what you do with the book," she said.

I wanted it to be like a movie, the mentor bidding an emotional adieu to a promising student. Here was the woman who was emblematic of my education, of my honing a passion which will course through me till my dying day. I wanted us to have a last cinematic interchange, directed by a sentimental ham like Spielberg: the violins swell, the shot goes grainy, a final talk freighted up with canned poignancy.

But nothing else was said. After a quick hug, we were done. The safety of my Tuesdays and Wednesdays was gone.

———

A swanky literary agent said she'd sell my novel in three weeks. I'd queried ten agents, give or take, and I got lucky: On the same exact day I got interest from one at ICM and another at William Morris, the two biggest talent hubs. I talked to both on the phone and decided to go with the woman from ICM—let's call her Liz—who was very maternal and warm over the phone, and I was a sucker for that.

"Three weeks, really?" I said.

"It's that good," she said. Liz was a legend in the business. She had a bunch of heavy-hitter clients, and I felt honored to be on her roster.

About a month later, I flew to Manhattan to make her acquaintance, to have meetings with prospective editors. I was to meet Liz at a restaurant on a Friday evening.

"What do you look like?" she had asked earlier in the week. "So I recognize you."

"I have a bleached Mohawk and a broken hand," I said. The

hand was a casualty of a late-night stupor-turned-tantrum that ended with me punching a kitchen cupboard.

"You really look like that?" she said.

"Yup."

"They'll love it."

Before I left to meet her, I got to thinking about Liz's assurance about how quickly she'd sell the project to a publishing house, so I did the only levelheaded thing I could think of: I quit my job.

I thought, *three weeks is nothing. I've got some savings. I can quit and in less than a month I'll strike it rich with a lucrative publishing contract, my working days are over, things are finally breaking my way!*

My meeting with Random House was promising. The editor there really dug the book, but had editorial suggestions that she'd need me to implement before her higher-ups would let her bid on the book. I liked her and the idea of a first novel coming out with RH was every author's dream, so I said, "I'll see what Liz thinks, and if she's cool with it, let's do a draft together."

Liz said, "It's a win-win for you. Either Random House buys the book, which is great. Or you get to do a rewrite with one of their editors, and we can take it with us as we hunt."

I ended up signing an exclusivity deal with RH to do this draft. I had about two months. The editor sent me ten bullet points to work on during the rewrite. Six of them were fantastic suggestions, and I knew exactly how to implement them. Two were okay, and by that I mean, yes, she was identifying problems in the book, but her ways of tackling them weren't right. The final two bullet points were only *bullets*. She wanted me to take them and blow my book's brains out, lobotomizing the thing.

I told her I couldn't live with myself making changes I didn't believe in. Then she refused to buy it. Once Random House passed, very quickly every other publisher passed, and Liz, who knew she'd be able to pimp it in three weeks, threw her hands up: "Oh well," she said. "We tried."

Oh well?!

We tried?!

"What now?" I said.

"Write another book," said Liz.

I did, but she didn't dig the new novel I wrote. In her defense, *Termite Parade* is a pretty angry story. I wrote it quickly in an amphetamine fit. I can feel the cocaine coursing through every page.

"I'm not the one to champion you going forward," said Liz.

"Huh?"

"You need a true believer to champion your work and foster the audience you deserve."

Champion should never be a verb, by the way, unless you're a serious asshole.

And that was how she fired me, with those glitzy euphemisms.

I sulked for a day, a week, a month—I can't remember exactly, but I assume I milked this setback for all its boozy worth. Finally, a friend from graduate school worked for a local lit agent in the Bay Area and asked me to send both novels. The agent went out to a cluster of houses, including an indie shop called Two Dollar Radio. I signed a two-book deal.

———

So five months sober on my first book tour, and that antagonist, *confidence*, crackling propaganda, telling me that I'll be fine, I can handle it, just go enjoy traveling around and talking about books, go ahead and sit around people cocktailing and you'll be all right.

I hadn't factored being around other authors I'd long admired. Like Joe Meno. He wrote *Hairstyles of the Damned* and was an indie lit rock star. He and I were scheduled to read together at Powell's Books in Portland. A magazine had asked me to interview Meno about his new novel so he and I decided to have dinner before the event to chat.

So I was anxious and excited, which really meant fidgety and sweaty.

It was one of those bistro pubs, all mahogany and burgundy and brass, like what I imagine dining on the *Titanic* would have been like.

Joe and I took a seat, and a server said, "Can I start you with cocktails?"

"Maker's and soda," said Meno.

"Me too," I said.

Wait.

What?

It slipped from my mouth effortlessly, an actor reciting a line well into a show's run, tongue trained in muscle memory to enunciate so every seat could hear.

Me. Too.

All I did for the next few minutes was loop that decision.

"Maker's and soda," he said, and I said, "Me too."

"Maker's and soda. Me too."

maker's and soda me too.

maker'sandsodametoo.

The server returned. Joe picked up his drink and said, "Cheers," and I held mine and said the same and we let our squat glasses touch and he had a taste of his and I excused myself to the bathroom.

Don't be stupid, proud, naïve. Just tell him you don't drink.

But I wanted to taste that bourbon, wanted to sip an army of drinks, would have drank the spills and sludge from one of the bar's floor mats if I could. There I was in the city of roses with a beast made of bourbon, waiting on my bistro table and me trying to pull it together in the bathroom because I had to be back out there soon, couldn't hide forever, no chance, I had to go fight that beast, because that was what happened at the end of fairy tales, heroes fought their enemies, heroes bested their adversaries. None of those tales ended with a hero hiding in the john dodging the showdown.

So:

"Or you could take that drink," something said to me.

It was one of my ghostwriters talking, my whiskey elves. My beasts. They were in that pub's bathroom with me, perched, one on each of my shoulders, as I leaned down to splash water on my face. Their heavy claws digging into my skin. Their feral, wide eyes fixed right on me. Their rabid jaws snapping as they made a terrible mewling noise. All the shrill squawks morphed into syllables and the beasts started making sense, telling me that this ridiculous sobriety of mine could be over, thank the lord, we could get back to doing what we knew how to do, stop pretending that we were something we were not, we could lie on the floor like ecstatic road kill, forgotten and splattered and dead.

"Doesn't that sound nice?"

"I want to stay sober," I said.

"We wouldn't be here if you did," they said.

They snarled again, mewled again, and I buckled. It wouldn't be so bad having a drink. It wouldn't be the end. I could stop at one. I could stop at one like a normal person.

They steered me back to the table like the worst designated drivers in the world, and Meno said, "You all good?" and I said, "My stomach," and he made a face like *that sucks*, and I was in my chair and I looked at the table and saw that bourbon and soda, and picked it up. A glass of fire in my hand. Under my nose. The smell of Maker's, that peanut and caramel scent. The smell of sanctuary. A quick tip of the wrist and I would be all right again.

One of the beasts said, "Down the hatch!"

And Meno said, "Should we start the interview?"

And I just sat there.

And the other beast said, "Down the hatch is code for drink your drink."

And I just sat there.

And Meno said, "We have to be at Powell's in about an hour."

And I just sat there; I just died there.

That there could be a future without booze felt impossible.

That I could do the right thing felt impossible.

That I could amount to anything more than a drunk felt impossible.

That I should expect anything other than relapse felt ridiculous.

That I could clutch a glass of bourbon.

That I could keep this stupid secret rather than just saying, "Joe, I don't drink."

That I felt so ashamed of being sober.

So uncool.

So un-whatever.

That I was willing to risk it all. That there was any hope that my *once upon a time* could lead anywhere but back to the bottom. That there was any hope with a drink in my hand. That there was any hope.

But I could put the drink down. I could put the drink down and turn on the Dictaphone. I could put the drink down, turn on the Dictaphone, ask Joe questions.

I could live, not live happily ever after, but the first word. Just *live*.

I set the bourbon back on the table and said to Meno, "Where should we begin?"

———

I checked my Dictaphone, and the interview with Meno is still on there. I listened to the whole thing right now. About forty-five minutes of conversation. Two writers talking shop, bullshitting about books. Normal. Not sure what I was expecting, some horror movie soundtrack? Shrieks. Pleads. The terrible mewling of my beasts, clues of how close I came to screwing up my life, but the tape held no evidence.

Just questions. Answers. Even some jokes. There were no noises of my almost-relapse. You couldn't hear any of the night's true chaos, because it all happened in my skull. It reminds me when someone in rehab said, "The biggest battles of my life have been fought in my mind. Fought with myself."

And what does that sound like on a Dictaphone?

Nothing. Dead air. The sound of deep space. A lonely hiss. No one hears the wars in your head. Except you. So you keep that Dictaphone recording. You listen to it because you know what's really there. Because you know that your beasts live inside the hiss.

———

I wonder if this book emits its own hiss. What happens when you hold it to your ear? Can you make out my scorched music?

6

FOR THE FEW WEEKS AFTER THE PEEK-A-BOO fiasco I carry around all sorts of selfish fantasies about copping and drinking, and because the world's rising oceans are polluted with irony, something unbelievable happens: I *have* to relapse.

I need surgery that will require opiate sedation.

In the junkie community, it's called a freelapse. You relapse, but it's okay. You get a free pass. You're supposed to get high, just following the doctor's orders.

I'd been praying for drugs and alcohol since seeing Ava fall, and a wicked god heard me, granting my wish with one malicious twist.

———

Which brings us back to where we started: Six in the morning, New Year's Day, me retrieving Ava from the crib and bringing her back to bed, the three of us lying like a happy family, then the numbness starting, no feeling on the right side of my body, from shoulder to toes, and me saying to Lelo, "911," and me saying to Lelo, "It's happening again," and she says, "What?" and Ava crawling all over me, yelling, "Hop on Pop! Hop on Pop!"

The night before, we'd been on a nearly empty New Year's Eve flight from Seattle to SF and I said to Lelo, "I hope 2015 is better than 2014."

"Me too," she said.

"It has to be, right?"

But eight hours after the flight, I'm numb and Lelo snatches the phone fast, propelled into action with desperate tunnel vision because we have some unfortunate experience in situations like these: Three years earlier, we went south from our home in San Francisco for the *Los Angeles Times* Festival of Books. I was scheduled to sit on a panel with some other indie press novelists and heard a popping noise in my head and lost the ability to talk, ended up at a Hollywood emergency room on a Sunday morning. After a CT scan, a chest x-ray, and an MRI, we were told the terrible news. I had a stroke. I was thirty-five years old.

And actually, I hadn't just had one stroke. The MRI showed a lesion on my brain, a scar from a stroke in my past. When I mentioned my enthusiastic drug history to the neurologist, she said I probably had the first stroke when I was loaded and might not have known. I imagined myself sitting at a dive bar, coked up and twisted on whiskey, and stroking right there, surrounded by other sorrow machines, me speaking in tongues, brain curdling, and no one noticing, including me.

Once Lelo and I traveled back north from Hollywood, over the next few months, my neurologist would run a gamut of tests and eventually shrug her shoulders. She'd note a ubiquitous heart defect called a patent foramen ovale, or, PFO, say it's nothing to worry about, it's found in twenty percent of the population. She'd say, "The stroke seems to be an anomaly. Take a baby aspirin every day and hope for the best."

I didn't know this at the time, but it wasn't an anomaly, nor did I have a PFO.

———

Years before: It was Christmas morning and someone was dead. A suicide on the tracks. I was stuck in the BART station, and service was stopped. Till the body was collected. Eleven in the morning and I had another cocaine hangover.

"The delay will be at least half an hour," someone said over the intercom.

I was on my way out to my step-mom's house. My sisters were already there. My dad wasn't. We were trying to celebrate without him. He'd been dead two years and it wasn't getting any easier. I didn't go to his grave anymore. Felt some obligation to schlep up there for the first few months after he passed. I'd sit and pick weeds from his headstone, try to talk to him but everything coming out of me was bullshit, saying he'd be proud of me like when I buttoned up his rented tuxedo shirt.

I was so sick that morning in the BART station that I couldn't sit. I had to pace, do laps around the underground platform, keep moving or die.

"Cleanup crews are working hard to rectify the situation," said the intercom.

The night before, Shany and I had gotten two grams for Christmas Eve. She was a Jew so the date was meaningless. Plus, Michael had just dumped her, screwing a bartender at one of our favorite watering holes. Shany was going to party and something as insignificant as the calendar wasn't going to stop her.

I'd known Shany since the tender age of nineteen, when we both got jobs as bussers at this waterfront restaurant. It was an instantaneous friendship and we were roommates for years. Recently, we'd started talking about the nineteen-year-old us. How simple and easy we had it back then. How free.

That Christmas Eve, I was on my own for a few days, Lelo up in Seattle visiting her family. I had my own reasons for wanting to get high: namely, I didn't want to go out to Sarah's, didn't want to be there, around my dad's absence—if you can be around an absence.

All night, Shany and I shot pool and did rips. Talking about that bastard Michael. Talking about how everything got worse with time. Wishing we were those nineteen-year-old fools again, new to San Francisco, so obliviously happy.

"What happened to them?" Shany said.

"Yeah, where'd we go?" I said.

We did another line, ordered another round of whiskeys.

I remember that we couldn't think of a single thing to cheers about. We held our shots up, racking our brains for something to say. Finally, we just drank.

In the BART station, all I could do was walk in circles on the underground platform and wait for every piece of that dead body to be collected off the tracks. Truthfully, jumping in front of a train wasn't the worst way to go out. You wait till it's almost on top of you. Then you dive.

You don't get high on Christmas Eve.

I didn't want to be en route to the dead man's house because I didn't want to be around people who loved me. I couldn't kiss my sisters or Sarah, couldn't feel their affection. I didn't even have Christmas presents.

It was good that other trains weren't running right then because that coked-up Christmas morning was the first time I actually thought about suicide.

"Service should be restored in another half an hour," the intercom said.

I kept circling, staggering around the platform, wishing I had that ill-fitting and faded Black Sabbath shirt from that other Yuletide disaster. It was better than being empty handed.

Lelo summons emergency services, and it's not the same ambulance, not the same EMTs, and no one gives me a bear in scrubs, but nevertheless we speed to the hospital and my symptoms get worse, affecting my vision, my speech, and the guy asks me questions in the back and I'm having trouble talking, producing these horrible moaning noises that don't mean anything and he averts his eyes, tells me not to worry about it, and then we are at the admittance desk at the hospital and I'm being asked the same batch of questions, along with some forms that I'm supposed to fill out, clipboard thrust at me as I lie on the rolling gurney, I'm supposed to start by writing my name and address and the like but my brain is broken, the pen won't work—I try to spell J-O-S-H, knowing full fucking well that the second letter of my name is O, so why did I write down a W? why can't I remember how to make an H? and the nurse takes pity and says she'll write these things down for me if I tell her the info, though trying to speak is still distorted, garbled, the words "San Francisco" take forever to fall out of my mouth and the nurse taps her pen.

———

After that Christmas morning in the BART station, I started to tell time differently.

Eight in the morning, and Lelo left for work, and I was unsupervised till six. Ten hours alone, idle in the Mission with all the bars.

Best case scenario was I wouldn't have a drink till she got home, and then I'd whisk her away to happy hour somewhere, say the Latin American Club or The Lone Palm or The Attic, and we'd talk about her day and I'd lie about mine and she'd nurse one or two drinks while I tossed twelve, a look on her face like someone stranded in the rain without an umbrella.

Keep in mind, those days were the best case scenario; I was steadfast, resolute—no booze till she got home. Distractions: going to the gym, sparring with some guys, running miles, writing. These were sober days I felt proud of, and truthfully, I have no idea why I was able to stay clean on these mornings, these afternoons. What made Monday a sober one, while Tuesday was a blackout? I'm not sure, but I do know that drinking with Lelo always felt like celebrating, awash and kept warm in her smile's light, while the cocktails I had by myself hit my mouth like spoiled milk.

But those *other* days, the soured ones in which I didn't make it till she got home—during these, there was a vulgar clock that told time by vices. Lelo leaving at eight a.m. Me drinking a beer. Loved drinking in the shower. Pop a tall boy and stand there with the lights out, that contrast between a cold beer and the scalding stream was heavenly.

By nine, these mornings were all rock and roll, music blaring, doing lines by myself if I felt like going up, or throwing back a pill if I wanted to get that opiate thrum going, the buzz starting in my feet and slowly swelling up around me, like living inside an electric toothbrush.

By ten, it was time to socialize. These outings always began at Clooney's. It's since been fixed but back then, the neon sign outside had a malfunctioning C. So it said *looney's*. Our insane asylum. What can I tell you about that bar? Being there in the morning was like the emergency room on a Saturday night. An utter shit show. A pageant of debasement. Everyone was in various states of injury, defiantly celebrating their damages with drinks. People in wheelchairs, with walkers, on crutches. Casts, splints, bandages, eye patches, you name it. Drinks were so cheap that it attracted the worst of us. I met an African man one morning who had these weeping sores all over his face and I half-expected a bumble bee to land on his cheek, sucking nectar from those sick blossoms.

Behind the bar an old-timer worked the early shift. Often, I had a lined denim jacket with me, balled up in my arms because the morning beer made me sweat during the walk over. With the wool of the jacket exposed, one time the bartender smiled at it, bringing over a little cookie and asking me, "Does your wee doggy fancy a biscuit?"

He wore crazy-thick glasses, a prescription that might have matched his needs back in the sixties, but over the last half-century, his eyes required more help.

"My what?" I asked.

"Your wee doggy," he said, nodding at the wool on my coat.

"That's a jacket."

His enthusiasm buckled. He dropped the cookie on the floor and retreated back to his post. When I sat down on a stool he pretended like we hadn't been conversing about my jacket/doggy thirty seconds earlier. "What can I get you?" he said.

By noon, it was time to have lunch so I'd meander to one of the Irish bars, maybe Liberties or the Phoenix, eating a burger and drinking wheat beers. I'd tended bar in the Mission for so long that I knew everyone in the business. These day-drunks weren't expensive, never putting a dollar in the till, just tipping my friends.

At three, I'd walk to Mission Bar where Ross worked the afternoon shift. I'd sit there before it opened, drinking Tecate from a can, the two of us bullshitting while he stocked liquor and cut up citrus. Every ten minutes or so, we'd have a shot, me hoisting Fernet, Ross doing rum. He was the only bartender I'd ever met who willingly put rum in his mouth.

Getting near five o'clock, the day would end one of two ways—either I'd brown bag it, getting a twenty-two of Pabst and sitting in Dolores park, people-watching, resenting how easy they made life seem while pushing babies on swings.

Or I'd go to Birite, the local market on 18th and Guerrero, buying supplies to surprise Lelo with a meal. I loved to cook; it made me feel better about myself, doting on her as best I could. Sure, I was wasted all day, but I could cook for her. I could sear a scallop. I could perfectly grill a rare steak. I could present these meals to her and think: *I am a dependable and caring person.*

―――

By the time I change out of my clothes, get some preliminary tests done, my physical symptoms have all subsided. No numbness. My speech is normal.

The on-call neurologist is a young guy. Too young. Younger than me. I want gray hairs. I want crazy wrinkles. I want his eyes to say *I've seen it all.*

He orders a batch of tests, imaging to make sure my brain isn't still bleeding, which it's not but the pictures do confirm that I've had another stroke.

I say, "That's three."

And he gives me the same pitying face as the admittance nurse.

―――

I am wheeled up from emergency a few hours later, loaded into the stroke ward. It's me and a bunch of eighty-year-olds, and each new hospital worker, every orderly and nurse and doctor, all say the same thing upon seeing me for the first time: "You're so young."

It becomes a chorus, and they don't mean it in a cruel way, but that's how I'm hearing it. *You're so young, you must really deserve this, that's the only reason you'd be here.*

At least I don't have a roommate. It's in the afternoon and because it's New Year's Day, there are a bunch of college football games on and I try and watch but my head hurts and I nap, fading in and out.

My step-mom relieves Lelo of any Ava duties at home, so my wife can spend time with me, bring me supplies, a pillow, a blanket, some books. Things to make this room feel less, well, like this room feels: a place where eighty-year-olds have strokes and die.

We watch football and try *not* to talk. We are both scared. Lelo is worried about becoming a widow. I am terrified that I'm going to have the *big one* any minute now, and Ava will have no idea who I am—or was.

My daughter and I have had so many moments together, so many milestones, that afternoon her feet first felt the ocean, a bite of pizza, hearing Jimi Hendrix on vinyl. Her inaugural sunrise—the two of us bundled up on our apartment's roof, after I'd just gotten home from a red-eye—and we watched the sky spill color, hugging the whole time. The two of us singing "Frère Jacques." Playing princess, taking baths, tea parties, boiling macaroni, putting stick-on tattoos on her arms so she looks like Daddy.

All these vignettes will die along with me. I don't remember anything from being eighteen months old. She won't have access to our cache of memories; I'll be a figment, a fleck of useless history.

Lelo and I stare at some stupid college football game, trying to hide our fear but it's not working. How can it be? We gaze at the screen like it's broadcasting the cause of my strokes and how to fix the problem.

My mind retreats to a memory, a Thanksgiving before Ava was born. Lelo and I got a cabin in the foothills and spent four days barricaded away, working relentlessly on our books. On the way up, we ate holiday-inspired turkey sandwiches in the car, but besides that, the weekend was dedicated to scribbling.

And so much laughter!

The ground had a fresh dusting of snow and each morning we'd play Frisbee out front of the cabin, holding steaming mugs of coffee while winging the disk back and forth. We talked about our novels. I loved how important literature was to her. Loved how *possible* it felt to someday succeed as an author around that infectious hope of hers.

As I sit in the hospital bed, the memory is clearer than any football game. I can see her standing on the snow, smiling as the Frisbee made its way to her, catching it, winding up, tossing it back, the plastic cutting its arc through the thin mountain air.

I would give anything to be back there.

Another nurse comes in to draw more blood. "You're so young," she says, sticking me.

————

I get a roommate late that night, Mr. Zhao arriving about two a.m. Lelo is long gone. It's been only me tossing and turning in this hospital bed, periodic visits from the nurse to check my blood pressure, my heart rate, temperature, etc.

Mr. Zhao doesn't speak English and any time a doctor, nurse, or physical therapist needs to talk to him, a translator is called on the phone and these translations are broadcast over speakers in our room and seeing how the only "wall" that separates us is a curtain, I am hearing the translator's loud voice as much as Zhao.

At first, this pisses me off. Haven't I gone through enough today? Do I really need to listen to Mandarin?

Quickly, though, my feelings on my new roomie change. I realize that we're the same. No, I'm not old and unable to understand English, but I, too, cannot comprehend what's happening.

Somebody please whisper that this will all be over soon. For god's sake, say Ava will know me!

We are separated by a thin curtain. Zhao and his stroke on one side, me and mine on the other.

When our room clears out again, I speak to him. "I want to live. I really want to this time."

We sit in our flimsy gowns with our beeping machines and our damaged brains in a room reeking of death.

———

One day, not long after the BART suicide, after I stopped telling time by the clock, only cocktails, I made a pilgrimage to Columbus and Columbus.

At Vesuvio, my favorite North Beach bar.

This wasn't Kae's San Quentin; it was mine.

Seven in the morning, and I was finishing myself off from the night before. Or starting the next binge. I had no idea what I was doing, but I was partying alone again. That was happening more often: people not wanting to spend time with me.

Alone, meaning there was nobody on the bar stool next to me. There were a few other masochists drinking in the morning. A couple had briefcases and wore suits, on their way to the office, stopping in for a quickie to tide them till lunch. The other guy was like me, keeping his bender above water, drinking whiskey and ginger ale. I ignored him until I heard a noise like a rattlesnake, realizing he was shaking a bottle of pills back and forth and smiling at me. He was four stools down.

"Are you in need of medication?" he said, sliding slowly toward me, going from one stool to the next like a stoned frog hopping lily pads.

He was in his forties. Or twenties. It's hard to tell people's ages when they're boozing in the morning.

"What's in there?" I said.

Still rattling all those pills.

"Do you really fucking care?" he said.

The Rattler had me. I would have taken anything. He was a doctor and a priest and an angel and a mother.

He opened the bottle and dumped two pills in my hand. Then he tilted the bottle to his mouth and munched a couple. "Bottom's up," he said, slamming most of his beer.

"Bottom…"

But I stopped myself there. This had to be it. I'd been hoping to get here for a while.

The Rattler rattled his pills again. "It's going to get nuts soon, brother," he said.

I bought the next round, both of us switching to Bloody Marys, making the obvious jokes about tomato juice and vitamins. We made the kind of small talk you do while waiting to be nailed to your cross.

And I'd love to tell you what happened next. Love to tell you some adventure I went on with the Rattler. But the truth is I can't tell you anything else. One minute I was sitting at Vesuvio nursing a Fernet shot, choking down a terrible Bloody Mary that tasted like aluminum. One minute, it was Friday morning and the next thing I knew it was Sunday.

Most of the weekend gone.

Lost.

But I've thought a lot about that vanished Saturday, and this is what I think happened, what I'd like to think happened. This is my make-believe Saturday: The Rattler was wrong about the pills. They weren't nuts. In fact, they weren't even drugs. They were soul salve. You ingested a couple and suddenly all the things that made you ache dissipated.

I couldn't stop smiling and it was one of those contagious smiles that only certain people are lucky enough to have (Lelo has one) and all these people that I loved were with me. We were on a cruise ship, which was odd, seeing as how I'd never been on a cruise, but that doesn't matter, not on a make-believe day.

My dad was back from the dead, looking handsome like he did before the chemo and radiation, a full head of black hair. My two moms were there—biological and step—and not only were they getting along, they were dancing, dancing together! And singing a silly song, something like "You Are My Sunshine," and my two sisters were there and they had this look in their eyes like I'd never let them down, never blown them off at the last minute because I was too hungover to see them or too ashamed to crawl out of bed, and Lelo was there with that Frisbee from our Thanksgiving trip, ready to play catch with a look in her eyes that I might amount to something if only I'd get out of my own way, and all the friends that stopped returning my calls once my drugging got out of hand, all these wonderful people from my past were on this cruise ship. Shany and V and Kerrie and Michael and Marc and Sara and Latch and Jabiz and Anthony and Rick and Johnny and Calder and Loperena and Ben and Barrett and even Blue and a bunch of other hammerheads I haven't told you about, and yes we all had dreadful dance moves but it didn't matter, no way, we were out at sea, under a disco ball, under a full moon, under every star in the history of the world, we were dancing on the open ocean and we were alive and we loved one another.

But Sunday morning rolled around. Because no fantasy lasts forever. Let me tell you about that Sunday morning—the day I almost died—before going to rehab.

I had the Rattler's pills. There were still twenty or so left. Did I steal them? Did he give them to me? Did I hurt him?

I don't know.

Never will.

I certainly couldn't have afforded to buy all of them. All I know is that they were in my possession.

Or I was in theirs.

Someone was somebody's.

I was in a hotel room. I was alone. I was naked. I was crying. I walked over to the door. There was a sign on the back of it. That said, *Check Out Time.* Under it was supposed to be written a specific number. Ten or eleven a.m. Noon maybe. Instructions for when you had to get out of the room. But there was nothing.

And I was bleeding. From my asshole. A steady leak. The bathroom destroyed. Towels soaked and strewn on the floor. Towels died pink with water and blood.

I hadn't been raped. That's not what caused the blood. I'd have been able to feel that. No, this trickle of blood was from something inside. Something was wrong in my guts. Something was breaking or already broken and a body could only process so much before quitting.

Check Out Time.

Looked at my nude, disgusting, bloody body in the bathroom mirror and it was like being in a Francis Bacon painting, and I needed to get out, thought to myself: *Let's get on with this, no more benders, I have about twenty of the Rattler's pills left and am probably about to bleed to death anyway so why not pop all the pills and float away from all this lacerating sadness?*

Well, why not?

There was a warm beer on the bathroom counter. In fact, there were half-finished beers and various bottles of booze all over the room. I popped six of the Rattler's pills and drank straight from a bottle of whiskey and then finished three of the open, flat, warm beers and then went back into the bathroom to look in the mirror, spreading my legs so I could see every trickle of blood and for a couple minutes everything felt right, I was going to be free, going to make it out of this, going to survive this life in another way entirely, survive it by leaving it, and those calm moments were righteous moments, but they didn't last.

No, I got this feeling like a fish first pulled into the boat. That fish flopping on the ground, gills going crazy, panicking and puckering my little fish mouth because I wanted back in the water to live—LIVE!—and the only way I could shake this fish feeling was to fall down to my knees in front of the toilet and make myself throw up the Rattler's pills and that was exactly what I did, giving all those narcotics back, shooting them up my throat and there was blood in that, too, and I kept kneeling there and got embarrassed that I couldn't follow through with this—what was I holding on to, why was I resisting giving up on such a hollow existence?—and these questions sent me back to the Rattler's bottle to take another handful of pills and wash them down with more open, flat, warm beers and I got to enjoy another batch of calm, righteous moments before the fish feeling returned and I dropped down to puke again, and I did the same thing a couple more times, until all the Rattler's merchandise had been ingested and spit back up, swimming in the toilet with so much of my blood and so much of my heart, and that was when this naked crying person capsized.

PART 2:
THE FREELAPSE
(OR: DO ADDICTS DREAM OF
ELECTRIC SHAME?)

7

TESTS. MORE TESTS. EVEN A SPINAL TAP, THOUGH
they don't call it that anymore, now it's the euphemized lumbar
puncture. It still means that I lie on my side as they attempt to
drain fluid from my spine, an agonizing experience because the
doctor keeps "hitting the spaghetti."

"I don't know what that means," I tell him.

"Nerve endings hang down and look like spaghetti noodles,"
he says. "I'm brushing up against them."

"Can you not hit them?"

"I'm trying." He works the long needle into the base of my
spine, like he's trying to pick a lock. I'm getting the sense he's
not a gifted burglar.

"I thought you said this wasn't going to hurt."

"I'm getting past the spaghetti."

"Have you done this before?"

No answer.

"You haven't!" I say.

Just the needle sliding in and out of my spinal cord roughly.
Every time he "brushes the spaghetti" my legs kick involuntarily.
When I had my elbow tattooed, there was something similar,

sending showers of sparks hurtling to my feet. But this is a hundred times worse and I worry I might pass out.

"Almost in," he says.

But he's not. I'll endure his stumblings for ten more minutes. He does finally penetrate the spinal cord, the fluid slowly dripping out. He holds a small vial of it up for me to see. "It's clear blood," he says, though I see a shot of gin. "This will hopefully tell us why you're having strokes in your thirties."

———

Because I decided not to die in that motel room, I called Sarah and told her I needed help. I took the subway to her house in the East Bay and crashed. Waking up the next morning, her dog's snout was inches from my face, deadly breath blasting from his open mouth, as he scrutinized me like a shrink. I didn't like how Boots studied me, so I lashed out: "You're going to die soon. That smell coming up from your insides is horrible."

"You'll die too," said the dog. I hadn't had any booze or drugs in twenty-four hours and the withdrawal was starting to rewire the rules of the world. Boots kept on me: "I mean, aren't you tired of this life?"

"I'm getting my shit together," I said, sitting up on the air mattress.

"Uh-huh," he said, smirking, limping away to scratch at the huge growth on his side. It looked like a saddle bag thrown over a horse. Except his saddle bag was under his skin. It was a huge tumor.

Boots was a retriever mutt, fur the color of bourbon. He stood at the backdoor, waiting for me to let him outside. I thought about ignoring him, but realized if he relieved himself inside, I'd have to clean it up.

It was a little after seven in the morning.

I was set to start to rehab in an hour.

I opened the backdoor and he waddled outside, off-balance from the massive growth on one side of his body. For whatever reason, I followed him out.

The patio was beautiful. A rose garden. A trellis with blooming bougainvillea. This was the suburbs and after living my adult life in San Francisco's fog, it felt good to see the sun so early in the morning.

Boots nosed around some rose bushes and, after raising his leg, found a patch of dirt near the fence. He started digging, not digging like I'm-tunneling-out-of-this-prison. Digging what looked like a shallow grave.

"I knew it," I called over to him.

If dogs could thrust up their middle fingers, I would have seen his right then. Instead, Boots worked his paws in the dirt, moving more from his plot.

Sarah joined me on the deck, handing me a coffee.

"Is that his grave?" I said.

"I should put him down, but after losing your dad, I can't do it."

"How long has he been digging it?"

"A few months."

"Months?!"

"We need to leave soon," she said, shuffling back inside, and I watched Boots dig.

———

Okay, as the docs go through all their tests, they finally find the culprit causing all these strokes, my congenital defect. My heart is missing a wall.

I have an eight-millimeter hole (a dime is about one-mm thick, so imagine a stack of eight dimes). There should be a wall separating the two upper chambers of the heart. This partition prevents blood from flowing the wrong way, so if in fact you have a blood clot, it will hit this wall and be filtered through the lungs, hopefully dissolve on its own; that's the way it should work. But without this wall, there is an open border, a highway for clots to travel up to the brain.

A neurovascular surgeon will build a wall in my heart.

I will be under anesthesia, a lovely opiate called fentanyl.

I wanted to get high, so here's the universe honoring my request. That's the thing about lobbing vague prayers—what if they're answered by a sadist?

———

There is only one surgeon who does these types of heart procedures, called ASD closures, and he won't be able to operate on me for two months. What that means is that I will have to pump an intense, outrageous, and hideous combination of meds to keep me safe until the surgery, each pill keeping my blood "slippery." This is one of the doctors' buzz words. Slippery. They mean thin, something that can't clot, can't turn to ice, blood like vodka in the freezer.

Keeping my blood so slippery, of course, comes with its own risks. Such as bleeding to death. I am given a list of things I should not do on all these meds, and this list, this crazy list, makes me fear everything. Don't drive a car, says the list. In fact, don't ride in a car. Don't shave. Don't use knives. Don't exercise. Don't have sex. Don't floss your teeth. Don't cut your nails. Don't pick up the baby. Don't be alone with the baby. Don't sit for longer than an hour. Don't take a multi-vitamin. Don't eat kale or spinach—too much vitamin K.

Don't go outside, if it can be avoided.

These meds have a lot of side effects and I stumble around my life, top heavy, my head feeling like an old parking meter full of quarters. The worst is the diarrhea. I lose twenty-five pounds in three weeks.

Sarah and I drove to a town deeper in the East Bay that started with a V. Vacaville? Vallejo? All strip malls and stucco and fast food shops. There was a liquor store across the street from the rehab facility.

Since this was an outpatient program, Sarah told me she'd be back to get me at five. She was being very nice, driving me around, letting me crash on her floor, blowing up that embarrassing air mattress. I was in my thirties but it felt like she was dropping me off at elementary school.

Sarah was the person you wanted around if something went wrong. Not a lot of people would have shown me mercy at that point. But Sarah didn't even flinch.

"Say cheese," said the nurse, whipping out a Polaroid and snapping a pic of my face. This was in 2009, and I didn't know anyone still used Polaroids. She gave the picture a good shake.

"Why did you do that?" I said, annoyed that we'd just spent twenty minutes filling out forms, her asking all the gruesome details. I even told her about how much blood I'd lost over the last couple days. She wanted specifics, but all I could do was blame a blackout, that familiar feeling of a coffin lid closing over me.

"We take everyone's picture when they first get here," she said. "Then we show it to them later on. You won't believe how terrible you look."

"Thanks."

"We all went through this," she said, shaking my out-of-focus face in front of my eyes.

"Why is there a liquor store across the street?" I asked.

She smiled, nodding at me. "I don't know. Why?"

"No, I'm asking you."

"Oh, I thought you were telling a joke."

"No."

"Baby, there's always a liquor store across the street," she said, then held the picture up for me to examine. "So what do you think of this guy?"

"I'm not a fan."

———

Leading up to the heart surgery, I'm saying all the right things publicly. These doctors are the best! The surgeon has done over 600 of these procedures! They are going to knock this out of the park!

Can't you see all my enthusiastic exclamation marks!!!

But there's a different discourse happening in my skull, various voices expressing a fundamental chorus: *I don't want to die.*

I try to assuage this fixation by learning all I can about the procedure and the man who invented it, Doctor Werner Forssmann. He invented this technique in the 1920s and couldn't get funding or any grants for research so he actually did this *to himself*, running a urinary catheter through the vein in his arm all the way into his heart.

Imagine that reckless conviction, that suicidal ambition. Imagine believing in something so much that you risk your own life. Forssmann must have known that despite his hypotheses, there was the chance his heart would give out as the catheter bumped through the vein and into the organ. And it wasn't enough to simply do the crazy thing. No, it had to be documented, which meant that he had to walk down a flight of stairs with the catheter wedged in his arm and pushing all the way to his heart—so he could get an X-ray, an image to prove that he was right: a picture showing the world what could be done, a catheter running sixty centimeters, from his arm and ending up in his right atrium.

When I think back on that night in the hotel room, my *Check Out Time*, I wasn't risking everything to make the world a better place. I was trying to turn something off, a sieve of indifference. Forssmann did this crazy and brave and unthinkable act in his mid-twenties, would win the Nobel Prize much later in life for this advancement. I can't think of my heart without thinking of his.

He's obviously to be praised for pioneering this procedure, yet he was also a member of the Nazi Party, one of their doctors during World War II. It's such a complicated question: What makes a good life? Here is a man, who for one shining and transcendent moment changed the way we operate on the human heart, paving the way for pacemakers, angioplasty, valve repair, saving countless lives.

But he was a Nazi.

Good life, bad life?

I've told you terrible things about myself in this book, and while I'm not a Nazi doctor, I do question my own worth. Ask any rational adult, she'll admit such moments of cataloguing positive versus negative contributions in life, and nothing makes you ponder your own identity, its value, your role in the human condition more than a health scare.

I start to talk to Forssmann. Why? Well, it makes me feel better. He is my angel, my tarnished and shameful angel. I feel if I speak to him, he'll watch my back, keep me safe.

One morning, I'm at the stove, frying an egg, watching it twitch and flop in the pan, hearing its hiss, but my mind is focused on the surgery. I've already burned the toast, tossing it in the garbage, the room reeking of bitter char. My goal had been an over-easy egg, though that's lost. Maybe I can salvage over-medium?

"You should have cooked it with a blowtorch," someone says, though I'm home alone. I turn around, and there he is, my savior, Dr. Forssmann. He's been dead since 1979, but it's his young self that visits me, a handsome, dark-haired twenty-something. He stands there wearing a white lab coat and says, "Give me the spatula." I hand it over, and he gently pushes past me. "Tell me, what did this poor egg ever do to you, Josh?"

"I can't imagine seeing you is a good sign," I say.

"I can't imagine how gummy this yolk will taste. Go sit down." He carries the pan to the sink and scrapes out the egg, then puts a heap of butter in, cracks another into the pan's center with a sizzle.

I walk to the kitchen table. "I'm not even hungry."

"You need your strength."

"Will I survive the surgery?"

Forssmann flips the egg over. "Do you know why I did it?"

"What?"

"Watch this." Using the spatula, he jimmies the egg from the pan to a plate and slides it in front of me. Then Forssmann sits across the table and rolls the sleeve up on his white coat. From his pocket, he produces a knife and a catheter connected to a long tube. "Are you squeamish around blood?" he asks, not waiting for an answer. I'd noted a similar pattern with the neuro-vascular surgeon who would be doing my procedure, during our initial consultation: He lobbed queries about my meds, my sleep, my state of mind, never hearing my responses out before barking his next inquiry. Surgeons, I guess, hold scalpels, not hands.

With the knife, Forssmann cuts himself on the elbow crease, accessing the vein, a few red trickles leak onto the table, too close to my eggs. "Eat up," he says, using the knife to point at the plate.

"You shouldn't bleed all over someone else's kitchen."

Then he feeds the catheter into the incision site, slowly snaking the tubing up his arm, across his shoulder, and into his heart, periodically grimacing but calm. Finally, Forssmann leans back in his chair, wipes sweat from his brow.

"I've done bad things," I say. "I deserve to die."

"Surgery is simple," says Forssmann. "Living with yourself

is the brutal aspect of being human. Trust me on this: I have a Nobel in Medicine, but I also have one in Remorse."

"Your bedside manner leaves a lot to be desired."

"Bed? We are in a kitchen," he says, ripping the catheter from his arm and bunching it in his coat pocket, a slow red stain blooming through the fabric. He ambles through the door, leaving me alone at my bloody table.

―――――

I was one of two people coming into rehab that day. The other guy was a kid basically. Barely twenty. Call him Trevor. He had this odd bleach job, uneven, bits of stark white mixed with brown hair, like somebody was peeling a potato and quit halfway through.

The first thing we went to was acupuncture. To help with withdrawal. We entered a darkened room with about thirty people sitting in a big circle. We took seats on the outside of the circle, next to each other, and waited for the acupuncture guy to get to us, to push pins in our ears. Then we all sat in darkness for forty-five minutes.

Maybe we were supposed to be meditating. I had no idea. I sat there thinking about Lelo—what this meant for us, would she wait for me, should she? Like Boots, I'd been digging my own grave and maybe the best thing to do was let Lelo leave so she didn't get sucked in too. Sucked down with me. Some graves have gravity, and she deserved much better. Blue had met a nice guy since we split and started a family. Lelo should have that same opportunity.

When the lights finally went on, the circle all stared at Trevor and me, waiting for Acupuncture to pull the pins from our ears. A little guy with blue hair pointed at us and said, "Welcome to the shit show, newbies!"

Then a bunch of us drove to a taco truck for lunch. To win

everyone over, I paid for all the tacos. "Next best thing to buying a round of whiskey shots," I said, holding my taco up like a
shot glass.

They hollered and smiled; we cheers'd with our tacos.

———

The surgery is scheduled for the mid-afternoon. I sit in the hospital bed, trying to watch TV. I post this on Twitter: "I'm having
heart surgery & as the procedure approaches, I'm getting scared.
Please send some good thoughts/prayers/healing vibes."

The outpouring of support is crazy. The indie literature community is tight-knit, but I don't expect so many notes. I refresh
my feed and read through so many wonderful comments and
they act as a salve.

Soon, a nurse comes over and asks if I'd like to walk upstairs
to the operating room or be wheeled. I walk. I make small talk
with him. A couple hours earlier, he had to shave my crotch, as
the doctors will need to access the artery in my upper thigh.

"Thanks for being such a gentleman," I say in the elevator. "I
usually don't go that far on a first date."

"My pleasure," he says.

———

Because I'd told the rehab admittance nurse about the anal
bleeding from the day before, I had to go to the emergency
room to get it checked out. Three IV bags of fluid to hydrate
later, I lay in a bed, waiting for the doctor to tell me I was dying.
Hep C or AIDS from sharing needles. All the unprotected sex.
Cancer from crappy genes.

I didn't know what was wrong with me, but I expected him
to come in wearing an executioner's mask. When he finally came
by—maybe an hour later—he had a disinterested look on his

face. He must have hated alcoholics. All the men and women hammering their bodies like piñatas. Except instead of prizes falling out of us, it was our organs, and we ended up here, on one of his beds, asking him to stitch our damage back up.

"You need to quit drinking," he said.

"That's the idea."

"No, your digestive tract can't take it anymore."

"Okay."

"Your GI is a mess, son. You have to stop."

"I am."

He looked at me like I was lying. Like he'd given this same advice to a thousand other piñatas who were back in a month or two.

"Know this is serious," he said.

And like that he was gone.

———

Forssmann holds the door open for me and the crotch-shaving nurse when we walk into the operating room. "Moment of truth," says Forssmann.

What's he doing mentioning *truth*? What am I supposed to do with truth so close to the surgery and the freelapse? I'll be okay. I'll survive. I'll just get high this once and that's it, back to being a husband, a father, a professor, a writer. This one needle going into this one arm one time doesn't mean anything other than that I'm following the surgery's protocols.

"Can I change?" I ask Forssmann.

"This life can be a misunderstanding."

"I'm not who I used to be."

"Maybe you are, though."

"I'm sober," I say.

"For another couple minutes, yes."

"I have to get high for the surgery."

"We are all Nazi doctors in one way or another."

I don't agree. Or I don't want to. People can learn, can grow. I have been fighting off a relapse for Ava and that's the key detail: I am trying to do the right thing.

But today, I have to do drugs to save my life.

Forssmann would point out the existential dilution, the good and the bad swirling through us, how in one life you can change the world inventing cardiac catheterization and then align yourself with a fanatical, murderous empire. He'd say it's the filthy order of the human condition, our strengths and weaknesses tangling together to spell our names, pump blood through our defective hearts.

The door slowly closes, separating us. I'm on the side with the operating table, the surgeons, the support staff, my future. Forssmann is on the other side, with its history and precedence, with his confusion and murder of memory.

———

As I waited in front of the rehab facility, Sarah's text only said this: *late*.

It was already ten after, and everybody bolted right at five. I thought there would be more people waiting for rides, smoking, complaining, withdrawing, but I was by myself.

I was staring at that god damn liquor store across the street. A beer—one simple cold beer—would do wonders right now. My head ached, my feet buzzed like they were asleep, I had that jet lag feeling. My body was tired of being deprived of all the liquor it was used to running on. Just one simple cold beer would take the edge off. And if I was going to do something stupid, why would I stop at one? Buy a twelve-pack and a fifth of whiskey and disappear.

"What's the good word?" said Boots, suddenly sitting right next to me, scratching at his huge tumor.

I nodded toward the liquor store. "I'm pretty thirsty."

The dog looked appalled. "Jesus, you're giving up after one day?"

"Mind your own business." Then I walked across the street, walked into the store, walked down an aisle, walked to the coolers, and just stared at all the beer behind the frosty glass.

I put my hand on the outside of the fogged window. It felt electric.

"Thing is you'll hate yourself," said Boots, now lying next to me on the linoleum, gnawing at his saddlebag.

Seeing him sprawled on the floor reminded me that I was sprawled on the floor, too, sleeping on that air mattress in Sarah's dining room. I was 33 and pretty much broke and pretty much broken and pretty much screwing up with Lelo and I'd gutted out my first day in rehab and the withdrawal sounded like basketball sneakers squeaking in my brain, and I was arguing with a dying dog in a liquor store.

"There's no reason for me to try," I said.

"This is my tumor," Boots said, glancing over his shoulder, "but those beers in there, those are yours."

I opened the cooler and grabbed a six-pack of tall boys. Thought about cracking one right there so the basketball shoes would stop squealing, but there wasn't time. Sarah would be there any second and I needed to split before she showed up.

I barely had any money, 15 bucks left after paying for all the tacos, so I'd need to break into someone's car or someone's pocket or someone's house... But then the harsh shame of pondering robbery made me want to crash down on the floor, use my fingernails like Boots used his paws, to tear up the linoleum and tear through the concrete underneath and tear up the building's foundation until I felt dirt, burying my body so everything would stop hurting.

I marched halfway down the aisle and stopped. I couldn't do

it. Jammed that sixer into a shelf of tortilla chips. Then I ran back to the rehab facility, sitting on the curb, panting.

"I'm going to screw this up," I said to Boots.

"You don't know that."

"It seems likely."

"I'm a dog," he said.

"Yeah, I know."

"You're lucky," said Boots, nudging my hand with his muzzle until I scratched his head. "You can put your tumors back. I have to ride mine all the way home."

We both saw Sarah's car approaching from a couple blocks away. She pulled in and smiled at me through an open window. "So how was your first day?" she said.

I got up off the curb and said to her, "One day done."

"Do you want to talk about it?"

I looked in the rearview mirror and Boots nodded his dog head—*yes*—from the backseat, letting me know his thoughts on the subject. There would always be a liquor store across the street, but I didn't have to go inside.

"What do you want to know?" I said to Sarah.

"Start with your favorite parts," she said, "and work your way to what scared the shit out of you."

And that was what I did all the way home.

———

On the operating table, I orient and calm myself by looking around at various lights, computer monitors, nurses. The anesthesiologist runs a line into the artery in my wrist. His needle, like an umbilical cord, pumps my favorite food.

This is it. I am relapsing. I am probably about to die. The surgery is minutes away. I've seen Lelo and Ava for the final time. My sisters. My moms. I've written my last sentence. These are the last moments of my life, lying here and looking up at the eyes of grumbling strangers, their mouths concealed behind masks.

"This first shot will be like drinking a beer," the anesthesiologist says, doing his merciful work. His needle brings the fentanyl. This is like seeing a long-lost friend.

Time loses its math, and everything gets heavy, oozy with smudged hues.

I am high again.

I am home.

8

WE HUDDLED AROUND A WRECKED MAN, GET-
ting as close to him as we could. This was in men's group, some-
time during my first week in rehab. All of us—say eleven or
twelve withdrawal machines—surrounded Mort as he whispered
his syllables, straining to hear everything. Mort had crashed his
car a couple weeks back without a seatbelt on and had crushed
his larynx on the steering wheel. He could only speak in whispers now.

There was talk about a surgery in a few months to fix his
throat, but Mort was thinking about not doing it, living like this
forever.

"I deserve it," whispered Mort.

"Why do you think you deserve it?" the counselor said.

"Because it's my birthday, and my kids won't talk to me."

Then he wept. No one knew what to say to Mort. Probably
because there were no honest words to soothe him. Most likely
his kids had good reasons for not speaking with him. Instead,
we consoled Mort with our body heat, staying as close to him
as we could.

For the first time since starting rehab, I was okay with being
there. Okay spending all day sitting in circles, okay spending

all night sleeping next to Boots on the air mattress. Okay with being away from my Mission District life with Lelo. Despite the agony of withdrawal, despite the anxiety for what a life without substances might mean, I moved with the other men toward Mort, our whispering sun.

———

A few days later, we were to write a poem telling our story, and the only thing I could think of was bedwetting. I know, not particularly poetic or pretty, but the counselor only gave us ten minutes so if that was where my mind wanted to go, bedwetting it was.

I was a serial bedwetter. Blackout drinkers were known to darken the sheets because we never remembered to piss on our way to pass out. So each bed in each apartment with each new woman, this was how I could tell my life story:

I wet the bed. I am twenty years old. I am alone. I am too drunk to care. I roll out of the soaked part, curl up on the edge, clammy, too useless to feel shame.

I wet the bed again and this time it's everywhere. I take a blanket and sleep on the hardwood floor. The next morning I don't remember doing it. I wake and think: now what the hell am I doing down here?

I wet the bed and somebody screams at me and I have no idea who she is, watch her dress in a hurry and head out so I shrug and settle back in. I couldn't care less about some piss. I'm going to shower in the morning anyway. What's the big deal?

I wet the bed and don't know it and Blue shakes me and says, "Jesus, you did it again," and I say, "Huh?" and she says, "Go to the couch," and I stumble down the hall. The next morning, she comes out and asks, "Are you still alive?"

I wet the bed again. I am alone again. I lie right in it and shiver. I should roll over, roll out of it. I should get up. Should crawl to the floor or

*the couch or the shower or the phone to beg for help. But I'm okay with lying
in it. Why on earth am I okay with this?*

I got the whole poem out in one burst and sat in my chair.
There was still six minutes left to write, but that was all it took
me, four scrawny minutes to sum up the last decade plus of my
life.

Ten years doused in urine.

I should've written a stanza about Lelo; she had felt me sully
a sheet or two. But there was no way I could include her. I was
hoping our stanza wasn't over.

———

We were told to tell a story of doing something nice. Just saying that word—*nice*—to a bunch of addicts brought out the
eye rolls and one-liners. Ask us to catalogue the nefarious and
we could trade war stories all day, but saying something kind?
About ourselves?

Despite our objections, we had to go around our circle and
share. The counselor waited for one of us to volunteer to go
first.

I thought of Jessa, a woman I had an affair with back before
Blue. On our first date we drank margaritas at the Latin American
Club and she said, "I'm pregnant." We waited tables together.
She had an outstanding sense of humor and a lewd mouth. And
she was strong. She swam out to Alcatraz on the regular.

"Who's the father?" I said.

She told me about this guy she'd been with—Chris?—and
how it had ended badly a couple weeks back. He gave her money
for the abortion. "But he won't come to the clinic with me," she
said.

"I will."

The day of the procedure, I sat out in the waiting room. I

thought there would be a swarm of uncomfortable men, pacing about like caged animals, but it was only me.

Eventually, the nurse led me back to Jessa. She reclined on a small bed, sucking a small can of apple juice. That look in her eyes. How can I describe that look? Jessa was ten years older than me, and I couldn't comprehend what an abortion meant to a woman. To me, it was some clean decision: You don't want to have a kid. I was too young to understand the churning complexities.

Anyway, that look: Her eyes were teary and distant. She was here and a hundred other places. She was happy and unhappy and taking care of herself and not taking care of herself and she was sure this was the right thing to do and regretting her decision. Jessa was the caged animal.

The only sounds in the room were the sips from her apple juice can.

Then I took Jessa to her apartment, got her in bed to nap. I asked if I should lie down with her, but she said it would be better if she were alone.

"But don't leave," she said. "Just be in the other room."

"That's fine," I said. And it was. An hour ago, she was pregnant. Now, she wasn't. I sat in the kitchen with a pot of coffee and a Kesey novel, *Sometimes a Great Notion*.

"Will you get me some McDonald's cheeseburgers?" she said awhile later. "I know that's gross, but it reminds me of being a little girl. Comfort food."

"It's not gross at all."

"Yes, it is."

"Okay, maybe a little."

She lived in the Upper Haight and there was a McDonald's about six blocks away. Once I'd gotten the bag of cheeseburgers, I hurried back. Feeling all empowered, all important. I couldn't wait to hand that greasy sack to her. I stormed into her room, holding the bag over my head, held it up like it housed the cure that would save her. Sure, those burgers didn't really mean much, but it was what she needed from me and I wouldn't let her down.

"Your comfort food, my lady," I said.

I hadn't thought about that day in years, but it seemed nice. I didn't want to go first, but the counselor waited for one of us to raise our hand. She needed me, like Jessa, and being needed was part of being human. That was why I was in rehab: to turn human again.

So I raised my hand.

She asked me to stand and share. I told them all about Jessa and the cheeseburgers, and a crazy thing happened: They gave me a standing ovation. I feasted on my own comfort food.

———

A couple days after that, we were told to take out our phones and delete every contact. People weren't having it. "I need these numbers," they said.

The counselor was prepared for our incredulity. Every new crop of addicts must have reacted the same way. He countered our protestations with, "Most of those people in your phone don't care about you. Delete everyone and make them earn their way back in. If they're good to you, reprogram their numbers. Otherwise, never talk to them again."

"Delete our parents?" someone said.

"Even them."

"My husband?"

"Yes."

"What about the Chinese delivery guy?"

"He'll understand," said the counselor.

I had over 200 contacts in my phone. Maybe some cells allow you to bundle and delete a bunch at once; I had this crappy old phone, which would only delete numbers one at a time. A bunch of the numbers were people I didn't even know, probably plugged in at last call, promises to drink together again. Others were restaurant and bartending buddies. Some belonged to old one-night stands from the days before I met Lelo, programmed not with their names but clues about their identities—*Diner, Green Eyes, Platforms, Pizza Place, Pig Tails, Vodka, Young.*

I deleted all these people.

It was harder to erase my family, of course—my mom, my step-mom, my sisters—but I wanted to get rid of everything that day. If it was possible I would have deleted myself. I was experiencing a grieving process in rehab, saying good-bye to the caveman.

I even deleted Lelo, hoping she'd call back so I could add her again. I wasn't confident, though. She was saying all the right things—*I love you and want to support you through this* and *I'll be here when you're ready.* But why would she wait? Why should she?

"Addition by subtraction by disaster," I said to myself, nixing another number, Watch's. Thinking about what we did that night, how we made the world a worse place.

———

Watch and I were chaos junkies. Lots of things were broken in our wake.

The night I need to tell you about happened years before I got into rehab. I'd love to say otherwise—that this horrendous act with Watch made me wise up, sober up—that it made me want to be a better person. But this was years before.

Watch and I popped pills and shot pool in North Beach. It was game seven of the NBA finals. A stranger walked up to us, saying, "Next round is on me. I just won $500 on the game." He pointed to a TV behind the bar where one basketball team was hugging and pouring champagne on each other, while the other team hugged and cried with no champagne.

"Winner winner, chicken dinner," I said to him.

"Huh?" he said, looking around the bar. He was white, in his thirties, dressed in ill-fitting and bland Costco clothes. "Chickens? Where?"

"It's an expression," I said.

"I don't think chickens belong in pubs," he said, pulling his cash from his front pocket. It was in his hand for a few seconds before thudding to the floor. The bills scattered down there. We could see a few hundreds and a wad of small stuff. He wobbled down to collect them. The guy was annihilated, standing back up and staggering a bit as he checked his six for rogue chickens. Watch and I smiled at each other, seeing someone who might subsidize the next couple hours of our cocktailing with his winnings.

It seemed important to agree with his anti-chicken stance in order to form a friendship. Watch and I both tended bar and knew the importance of indulging alcoholics their preoccupation du jour.

"I concur that liquor and poultry should be kept separate at all times," I said to him.

The guy nodded, then eyed Watch, awaiting confirmation of his allegiance as well. "Yeah, fuck chickens," said Watch.

This guy erupted into applause. "Exactly, men. It's not sanitary to have them flap about with open beverages around. Let's spearhead a movement to make it illegal to harbor chickens in any establishment that serves alcohol. Agreed?"

We agreed, of course, uh-huh, we'd never turn our backs on such an honorable cause.

He seemed satisfied: "Now what would you fellas like to drink?"

We ordered three whiskey shots with bottles of PBR. The bartender carried the whiskeys, balancing them in one palm. He carried our beers in his other hand, his fingers lodged in the necks of the bottles, bowling ball style. It was that kind of bar. You slipped your beer off the bartender's fat fingers and thanked him for it. Hoping, simply hoping, that he washed his hands after pissing.

"To winning all our bets!" the guy said right before we took our shots. "To being huge winners!"

———

Every session in rehab started with us going around the circle and introducing ourselves by our first names, saying what our drug of choice had been. Trevor always said, "I'm Trevor, and my drug of choice is MORE."

We laughed and clapped after he choked his catch phrase out, so imagine our let-down the day Trevor was called out by one of the nurses before the introductions. I was called out too. Once in the hallway, she ushered us to a back corridor I'd never seen. "I need a urine sample," she said.

"Why are we being singled out?" I said.

"Everybody does it during their second week. I'll be right back with your cups."

We sat down in the hallway. Trevor looked worried, so I said, "What's wrong?"

"Will wine show up?" Trevor whispered.

"You drank wine?"

"What about weed?"

"Of course weed shows up."

"But weed stays in your system for like a month," said Trevor. "I could have smoked it before I got here. How would they know when I got high, right?"

"Have you got stoned since we started?"

Trevor gave me a smile, a condescending one, and said, "My name's Trevor, and my drug of choice is MORE."

I was angry, almost felt betrayed. We were in this together. We were withdrawing together, opening up during group. We were prescribed Suboxone and trazodone. We smoked cigarettes. We were friends. That's what sticks out to me now—how much I liked Trevor after only knowing him a couple weeks. He was a good kid, and I was jealous of him, wishing I'd gotten in treatment at twenty years old, avoiding all that aching.

But maybe he hadn't lost enough yet. That was the problem of being young in rehab. He hadn't sacrificed enough people, hadn't dismembered every promise he made, hadn't doctored and botched his dreams, leaving them for dead. The rest of us had left no humiliation uninhabited.

"Why are you smoking?" I said. "We're here to get clean."

"I'm here for my parents."

"What if they kick you out of the program?"

But all he did was shrug. I can see him doing that gesture so clearly even today. Shrugging like, *oh, well.* Shrugging like, *what can you do?*

And if I could talk to him from here, I'd say this: We can do lots, Trevor. We can get our shit together. We can, for the first time in our lives, try and make things better. We can decide to live a good life, one with Lelo and Ava, instead of carousing with Watch.

———

Me and Watch and this guy—call him Wasted Winner—had played five or six games of cutthroat, killing a few hours. Wasted Winner could barely make contact with the cue ball. Watch and I were of the opinion that it might be simpler to cut out the middle man—i.e. the Wasted Winner—and absorb his funds.

Which is just a bullshit way of saying we were going to rob him.

Even years removed, thinking about what I did makes shame swell. I can say it only happened because I was drunk. Because of the pills. I can say that with a clear head I would never have acted that way, but do you really care about my reasons?

And do I?

"Would you like to get stoned?" I said to the Wasted Winner, who didn't even have to think about it, going ballistic like a dog seeing the leash in your hand, saying, "Should we smoke in the bathroom?"

"No, he lives around the corner," I said, pointing at Watch.

The Wasted Winner's tail kept wagging: "What are we waiting for?" Then he kept blathering about his luck, while we walked out front of the bar. "A lot of gamblers don't touch the NBA, but I've plied my craft," he said. "I'm an expert."

It was about midnight. No one else was around. There are a bunch of trees surrounding Coit Tower, so it was the perfect place. One thing you need to know about Watch and me: We'd soldered together the ugliest parts of ourselves, our hate and rage and regrets, the pulp of our broken hearts into one gigantic fist. And once our fist formed, there was nothing we could do to stop it. To stop us.

"We can take a short cut," said Watch, pointing up toward the Tower.

"You live up there?"

"No, I live right on the other side. This is a quicker way."

"Let's take a taxi," Wasted Winner said. "I am in no shape for cardiovascular activity." He looked around for a cab, and even though none were around, hoisted his arm and yelled *taxi!*

"There's a nice view up at the Tower, too," I said. "Winners should see this view."

He put his arm down. He smiled. He had no idea.

Maybe an hour after our piss test, I looked for Trevor. He was with a few heads outside, smoking cigarettes. "Are they kicking you out?" I said.

He ushered me away from the group. "They saw the weed, but I had it in my system when I got here. My plan worked. I'm all good."

"Why did you smoke last night?"

"I told you," he said, "I'm only here for my parents."

"Why?"

"Ask them yourself. They'll be here for family day."

"I'm not going to family day," I said, repulsed by the suggestion. Everyone in rehab had spent the past couple weeks splattering the walls with our secrets, telling all the shit we tried to keep from our families, and now these populations were going to mix? How? Why?

But that wasn't what I was scared of, not really. My real fear was that I'd ask Lelo to come and she'd refuse, too busy boxing my stuff up and leaving it on Valencia Street. Too busy finding a guy who could moderate his intake, who could come home when he said he would. She'd find a gentleman and they'd share a normal life, and she deserved it, deserved him.

That was one of the things I hoped to discover in rehab: Was it possible for someone like me to turn into *him*? And would Lelo wait?

"You have to go to it. They make you," said Trevor. "Any of your people coming?"

"No. Maybe. I don't know."

———

I asked and she said yes, and then there we were: Lelo and I in the parking lot, out front of the rehab facility. One of the old-timers, Paul, was out there too, all agitated, pacing around and kicking rocks and talking to himself. He'd been in about a week longer than me. My first day, he was withdrawing from oxy so bad that he was wrapped in a blanket, sweating and swearing and moaning.

"What's the matter?" I said to him.

"My wife, that's what," he said.

"This is my girl, Lelo," pointing at her, both Paul and me forgetting about this thing called manners. He didn't even look at Lelo, saying something about his wife skipping family day so she could go wine tasting in Napa.

"Wine tasting?" I said, all offended on his behalf.

"Well, she should hate me," he said, all offended on her behalf. "I'm a shitty husband."

We were all shitty in one way or another in rehab. Shitty spouses and lovers and friends and daughters and sons and siblings and fathers and mothers and drinking buddies, and like Mort, we'll be whispering our whole lives, gruff forlorn voices saying, *sorry, so sorry, I wish you'd never known me like this.*

———

A bunch of trees surrounding Coit Tower. Midnight. No one around. Secluded. The perfect place. To hurt someone. To rob him. To unload the fist we packed. So it can run rampant. Rampaging. Releasing our fury. Watch and I walking up the hill. About ten feet ahead of Wasted Winner. He was out of breath. He was staggering. He was sweating. I was sweating. Watch was probably not sweating, thriving on violence. Conversation petering out. Just trudging, panting men. The promise of getting high motivating each new step. At least for one of them. The other two malevolently motivated. And I liked punishment. Punishing others. Punishing myself. Didn't really need a reason back then. Punished myself because I was there. Wasn't that reason enough?

Thinking about that TV back at the bar. The basketball players celebrating. Pouring champagne over one another's heads. Guzzling the stuff. Spanking every ass in the room. Their huge smiles. The way they spoke in tongues. The whirling way they moved through the locker room. Hugging and frolicking and howling, "We won. World champs, baby!" I couldn't stop thinking about the champagne. How that must feel. How it must feel to have someone celebrate you. Your accomplishments. Your role. Your hard work. Your being on the planet. What must it feel like to have championship champagne drizzle down your face?

My only drizzling was adrenaline. Maybe a squeak from a run-down conscience. Some fear. Getting caught and going to jail. And for what? A couple hundred dollars? That's the thing—we didn't need the money. We weren't doing this for that. No. Trudges and pants. Three men moving. Toward emergency. Toward an anger apex. There's no such thing as divine intervention. No such thing as celestial protectors. Nobody intervenes. We are left to cripple ourselves. Mangle ourselves. Left to our own devices, we crumble to the occasion.

Nearing Coit Tower.

I said to Watch, "Now?" and he looked around one last time and not seeing any witnesses out there, said, "Now," and Watch turned and hit the man, who tried to say something but these syllables were muffled and busted, and he didn't fall down after the first blow so I hit him too and he went to the sidewalk with more muffled and busted syllables and we kicked him a few times and rifled his pockets for what was left of his winnings, ripping that cash away, and whatever we gained that night, say $200 split between us, doing all that damage for a hundred bucks each, what we took with us as we left that guy lying there had nothing to do with money. What we took was a stash of disgrace.

Wounds only we could see. Ones that wouldn't lighten with time like old tattoos. Remaining visceral and wicked and profound. Colorful and ornate and raw. Ones with fists of their own.

———

And there we were on family day, three weeks into the program. Us, the addicts. Them, the intruders. I don't mean to make it sound adversarial. But I sort of do. Because that's what it felt like: We'd been in a womb and now this was the first stirrings of labor, proof that we'd be birthed back into the world, and there was the chance that I could know life without being a caveman.

The worst part of having them there was how little they knew us now, assuming we stayed clean. They knew us as drunks, IV drug users, people who smoked speed using broken light bulbs as pipes, people who mangled promises, people who burned money like wicks, people who hit their loved ones, couldn't hold down a job, couldn't stay out of jail, couldn't love their kids. They knew our crimes and our lows and because they'd seen us at our worst, how were they supposed to give us the benefit of the doubt? And how were we supposed to give ourselves the benefit of the doubt with them around?

When it was just us, trying to make sense of a future without drugs or booze, that was one thing. But sitting amongst all the people whose hearts we'd gouged out—what gave us the right to expect better from ourselves, expect anything other than relapse?

We couldn't feel empowered sitting with these eyewitnesses for all our sins; like a suspect lineup, they could finger every last one of us. With them there, we were hopeless. Doomed. Preternaturally stupid. We'd never stay clean. Never amount to anything. We were swollen livers, shaking hands. We were DUIs, abscesses. We were violent nights with Watch.

Everybody sat in these neat little rows of seats set up in one of the conference rooms. If you didn't know better, you'd think we were there for a real estate seminar. Trevor and his parents were in the front row. I pointed him out to Lelo and said, "That's my friend."

"What's with that guy outside?" she said.

But I didn't want to talk about Paul or his wine-tasting wife. "See that kid up front? That's Trevor. Those are his parents."

"They look so normal," said Lelo.

She was right. If this was a real estate seminar, these responsible parents had taken their precocious kid here to learn the intricacies of flipping properties. They had no idea that he wasn't listening. They had no idea he wasn't interested in real estate or sobriety. He was only interested in MORE.

The guy running family day had a tragic ponytail running all the way to his ass. First thing he said was, "Does anyone know where the word *addiction* actually comes from? It's Latin. From the word *Addictus*. Meaning to devote yourself entirely. To worship."

To worship!

Think about that for a second. Think about this congregation of junkies and drunks falling to their knees and praying for their god's love, knowing that their deity required more than mere prayer, and so if you wanted to belong here, with us, you needed to speak with actions, show your devotion to this contagious god through debauchery and debasement, needed to wreck everything you held dear, destroy everyone who had ever shown you kindness, and once you were alone and broken, only then would you be allowed to crawl in our coffin, our cathedral, and feel the thrill of worshiping pure despair.

Addictus.

To worship.

To be a worshipper.

I looked to Trevor, sitting with his family, them having no idea that he still secretly worshipped MORE, them hoping that his presence here meant that he was ready for a better life, but he wasn't. He'd be back in rehab, hopefully, sooner rather than later. I looked back at Paul standing by himself, his family too incensed to show up. Looked at lowly Mort, whispering to himself. I so badly craved a future that wouldn't lead me back here.

I clutched Lelo's hand, maybe too hard, but I could barely control my limbs. Here was my chance to never hurt anyone again. I leaned over and said to Lelo, "I love you."

"I love you too," she said.

"I can be a better person," I said. "I'll show you."

"I believe you."

And we listened to Ponytail talk for about an hour. Not me, the mess. Not her, the family-day intruder. There were no divisions between us. I was wrong about that. No, if she was brave enough to walk in the room, then she was a part of this thing. And if Lelo was that strong, maybe I could be, too.

The two of us, the entire room of us, listening together.

9

THE FENTANYL KNOCKS ME INTO A TRANCE— how I've missed the feeling of a needle, of a drug pulling the bones from my body—and the next thing I know, I'm being awakened. The surgery takes about ninety minutes, though to me it feels like seconds. It is a success. My heart has the necessary wall, that eight-millimeter hole plugged up.

I'm groggy and still high as they wheel my bed downstairs. We are on our way to a test to make sure the procedure has worked. We stop by the waiting room so I can see Lelo. Very rarely in life, do you know with certainty that you are in the middle of a profound moment while actually experiencing something. Usually, we assign value to these things in retrospect.

But not this time.

Not seeing Lelo.

Not watching the most beautiful smile I've ever seen erupt on her face. She runs over to me, leans down, and we have a hug, the most perfect one. All her worries about me dying, leaving her a young widow with a baby, all of these qualms mutate into pure affection. She is relieved, and I am relieved, which feels like too casual a word, though it's what we are.

They verify if the surgery is a success by "bubble test." They shoot saline bubbles into my heart and hopefully, the bubbles hit their device, my new wall. If the bubbles can't get through to zoom around my heart's chambers, ambling this way and that like clouds, I'm fixed.

I lie there and watch the ultrasound machine. My heart is on the monitor, black and white, beating and repaired, and the bubbles hit the newly implanted wall. I know those are only bubbles made of saline, know that they are not in fact blood clots, yet that's what I see, a whole infantry of clots trying to cross through my heart and speed up to my brain, trying to take Lelo and Ava away, but they can't. They are blocked and I am all right.

I get to be a dad and a husband for a while longer. There are, obviously, no guarantees, but I'll make it till tomorrow. And if I'm lucky, I'll live long enough that we can walk through an entire garden of milestones, and I'll look back on a long life, one without another divorce or estrangement, one in which I bask in our luck: I survived three strokes in my thirties, survived an ill-formed heart, survived a procedure that saw surgeons entering and planting a device in my chest.

I say to the surgeon, "Everything's good?" and he says, "You're like everyone else now."

And he means it.

But he's wrong.

That opiate dose revives my caveman; I can feel his limbs stretch in me after a long hibernation, his stomach growling, famished for drugs.

———

The first time I shot special K I'd been at Becky's house, back in my early twenties. We worked at the same restaurant—her waiting tables, me behind the bar—and she'd been talking up

K, saying how it was the best high in the world, and wouldn't I like to try it?

Of course. I tried everything.

After work, we went to her apartment, and she introduced me to her weird Nordic husband, Olaf. He had long blond hair, matted and flat, the bedhead zombies had fresh from crawling out of graves. Olaf was something of an amateur astrologer, sitting in front of a bank of computers. Right after shaking hands he peppered me with questions about my birth. What city and state? What time? What day of the week? What longitude and latitude?

"Your true horoscope needs to factor in the vernal equinox," he said.

"I was born in a taco truck," I said, "right outside the Vatican."

Olaf stopped pecking at his keyboard, shook his head. "This is your life. Take it seriously."

Then Becky walked back in the room with a plate that had three syringes on it.

Immediately upon seeing her, Olaf stood up and dropped trou, pointing his pale butt at Becky. As opposed to heroin, which had to be shot in a vein, special K went into muscle. Becky took one of the syringes and jammed it in his butt cheek.

K was a liquid horse tranquilizer. Club kids cooked it down, baking it in the oven to a powder so they could snort it.

But some sickos shot it.

After fastening his pants, Olaf took a syringe and stuck it in the back of Becky's arm, in the tricep. They looked lovingly at each other. It was actually a pretty romantic moment. They could have been new lovers sucking the same milkshake through two straws, foreheads almost touching, in some 1950s diner.

Instead they were here.

Becky said to me, "Where do you want yours?"

I swiveled my arm around and she shot it in my tricep, too.

"Sit on the couch," she said. "You've got about thirty seconds till you can't move."

Being in a K-hole felt like falling from my consciousness, but not so fast that I was scared. The drug had a parachute, and I meandered through the clouds, the haze. I was in a warm sky.

Falling...

Yes, falling...

And then landing back in my life.

Back on Becky's couch. It was an hour later. Maybe more. They were watching *The Matrix*. They sat in a chair together, Becky curled on his lap, playing with that long zombie hair of his.

"How was it, Taco Truck?" said Olaf.

"More," I said, just like Trevor. "Let's do more."

———

After family day, after my few weeks of rehab were done, I was back in the Mission. Every night was movie night, and we watched weird combinations of films. French New Wave with Spaghetti Westerns. Gangster flicks and satire. Slapstick mixed with surrealism, actually pairing *Trading Places* with *Eraserhead*. Were we afraid of John Candy opening up for Ingmar Bergman? Will Ferrell for Truffaut? No, we were not.

We had to embrace every fart joke from the lowbrow, every banana peel, every time a fat person fell down. No matter how telegraphed these gags were, we laughed anyway, chomping on takeout food, always watching from bed, wearing pajamas, sleeping on wonton crumbs.

We had to endure the most stilted and arcane scenes from the other end of the spectrum, too. The highbrow blowhards. The turgid. The cranks. Filmmakers who thought pacing was for the feeble-minded and so they slogged on, one bulbous scene after the next.

I'm talking to you, Matthew Barney. What's your deal?

Lelo quit drinking too. Not that she was a drunkard, but she did it out of solidarity. It's the nicest thing anyone's ever done for me.

I'm probably not supposed to admit this, but I miss drinking with her. Not the hammerhead nights, but the ones where I impersonated a normal guy. I miss making her smile while we polished off a single bottle of wine and went to bed, though that didn't happen too often. I bet she misses that too. Granted, she doesn't miss what comes with it, me staying out all night, or all the rowdy antics—seeing me punch some sap in the face as we toured Sonoma wineries, watching me expose myself to an old woman on the street, having to sit in the driver's seat while I spider-webbed our windshield with a whiny fist, or all the other bullshit. No bottle of wine is worth bringing that back.

Lelo made several choices. She chose to date me even though I told her I had no intention of curtailing my partying. Chose to stay with me while I explored Columbus and Columbus. Chose to stay with me through rehab. Chose to ride with me into the peculiar, surreal domain of being newly sober.

On our first date—the first official date—we had gone to see a Tennessee Williams play and stayed in a hotel downtown after. We were naked, drinking scotch. Lelo looked amazing, blond curls and blue eyes.

I was dazzled by her optimism. Here was a woman who saw *good* in the world. Here was a woman who made me want to see that, too.

I remember saying to her that night, "I party harder than you do."

"I know," she said.

"I'm not going to stop drinking."

"Okay."

I'd never done that before—been honest from the get-go. Usually, I downplayed my vices as I reeled in women. But the way things had imploded with Blue made me want to try this thing called honesty.

Of course, in that hotel room, we didn't know we'd make it. We didn't know we'd date for seven years; I'd get clean; we'd get married; we'd have Ava. Thinking on it now, it doesn't make any sense: Why should we survive? Why do some relationships work while others with promise get mowed down? It's like the soldiers in World War II who stormed the beaches at Normandy. Some survived. Some died. There was no reason. It wasn't like the guy standing on your left was a worse or better soldier. That's just where the bullet went.

On paper, there's no reason why Lelo and I made it, but we did. We're here.

For the first three months clean, we watched everything, going to the video store, Lost Weekend on Valencia, and feasting on all sections. No film was safe. Nothing was off limits. We devoured three or four movies a day. One time there was some shitty action movie in the new release section that came with 3D glasses (this was 2009 so it seemed like a treasured anomaly). We nodded, knowing instantaneously that we had to do this. You would have thought we were stoned the way we laughed, wontonning our asses off, splattering our pajamas in dipping sauces. It was one of the worst movies ever. I mean, Brendan fucking Fraser was in it.

It barely looked 3D—2½D?—is that a thing?—but we couldn't pull our eyes from the screen. Not caring at all. 2½D was as close to real life as I was capable of right then.

———

For a few days after the surgery, I stay at my sister's place. Jess just lives a few blocks from us on Bernal Hill, and I need to take it easy. Specifically, I'm not supposed to pick up or play with

Ava, which would be impossible for me if we're around each other.

So I'm in Jess's guest room, spending much of my day thinking about drugs. I had been offered a Vicodin script to help with the pain, but I passed. If I took those pills I would for-sure relapse. I might anyway, but I would have zero chance of making it with a pill bottle on the nightstand, rattling like that pick in my guitar.

When I had first gotten out of rehab, watching all those movies, hiding in 2½D, I felt sure that I wanted to get clean and stay that way. It was hard, of course it was hard staying clean, though I felt steadfast, amped up on hope.

Yet after the freelapse, that's not true. That simple taste of an opiate supersedes everything else. It's what I think about, what I care about. Cravings like that aren't hints or whispers. They're pencils hitting palms. They're Nazi doctors.

They're Forssmann saying, "It's impossible to do the right thing for a whole lifetime. It's not our nature."

I have the worst insomnia at my sister's and Forssmann won't shut up. I lie in her too-soft guest bed and sweat and squirm, too weak to do anything. Normally, with a mind barking like this, I'd get to the gym. Lift weights or spar. Run ten miles. Punish myself in a pure way.

But I'm feeble from surgery and so Forssmann stands over me, trusses my brittleness up with his knots, holds me captive in fantasies.

"I don't want to tear this life down," I say.

"Of course you do," he says, laughing at me.

Would I like to be the kind of person who after successful heart surgery feels nothing but thankfulness? Would I like to swell with grace, knowing how lucky I am for this opportunity to heal and live?

Obviously.

It's not who I am.

I'm this skeleton stuck in his sister's guest room, angling to squander his life.

"Everyone will understand," says Forssmann. "No one will judge you. It's not your fault; it's the surgery's. Take advantage of this. Exaggerate the pain. Get that Vicodin script filled. Go on a run."

I don't sleep at all that night.

I get out of bed and make coffee about six in the morning, sit in my sister's empty, dark kitchen. Cardiology doesn't open until eight, and they'll issue the prescription. A dash to the pharmacy and I'm free.

Sip of coffee, check the clock.

Sip of coffee, check the clock.

6:27 a.m.

I can turn anything into a vice.

———

After that first shot at Becky's house, about six months passed in a K-hole. Each needle had a dream in it, and I fell into their worlds without the burdens of reality, rules, logic, like living in my own little Dalí paintings.

If I wasn't at work or out at bars, I was locked in my room, shooting as much as I could. Spending every cent I had on vials. Sharing needles, cleaning them out with bleach, but who was that fooling?

I lived with Shany at the time, and she didn't like me using needles. "Not in our house. It's gross." She did so much cocaine you could have used all the powder to pot a plant. So coming from Shany any debauchery-regulations were a joke. The major thing in our flat was the *no shut up* rule. Which meant that no matter what the other person was doing or how loud, how annoying, how illegal, you couldn't tell them to be quiet. So when one person partied, even if you didn't feel like joining, you got out of bed, cracked a beer, rolled up a dollar.

So all that made it hard for me to hear any ultimatum about needles.

"Look, I'm just experimenting," I said. "No big deal."

"You've been in your room for three days."

That seemed like an exaggeration.

I probably would have kept experimenting with K until it was all I did. No job or friends or future. Till experimenting was my whole life. Luckily, one day at work there was this brunette, a new hire, named Blue.

"I know you do K," Blue had said to me, "and if you want to date, no needles."

"Okay."

"I'm serious. That's the one rule: no needles."

"I promise."

"You won't be a writer if you're a junkie."

"I'm not a junkie."

"You can be Henry Miller, and I'm Anaïs Nin." That was the first time she had said that, mentioning them, mentioning us as them, the first of many.

"Nice to meet you, Anaïs," I said.

———

If you're a Nazi doctor, you do the drugs. You cop. You swallow. You drift away from your family. You choose the grim path. You choose to be alone. You choose to never be accountable. You choose to ache. No drug is strong enough to make you forget all the love that's spilled from your life.

And she'll track you down, despite you being a lowdown Nazi doctor. Ava. When she's 18 or 23 or 31. She'll find your ramshackle world and enter your dirty perch. It will be her mission to see you, to tell you that she hates you, that she's fine without you, to plead for answers, in the same useless way you pleaded with your own parents. Ava will know it won't do any measurable good to confront a drunkard, but she'll be compelled to see this through.

If you're a Nazi doctor, you don't answer the door. You spy her through the peephole and hide. She's not buying it. Knocking and ringing the bell, knocking and ringing until you answer. She's persistent and poised. You are naked and frail. You feel yourself afire with shame. You feel a sense of regret that's been tamped out for years but she's gasoline, lighting you up.

"Was it worth it?" she says, eyeballing you, her magnificent disappointment.

"What?" you say, a sloshing cocktail in your hand.

"We had everything," she says. "I mean, we didn't have much money, and you and Mom had to work hard, and I slept in a glorified closet, and you were overtired and always behind and always feeling frazzled and questioning whether you were doing a good job, but so what? We had a happy life, Dad, and you left us. Why did you give us away?"

Anything you say will be useless and so you choose (again, the wrong choice) to say nothing. To shrug. To take a sip of that sloshing cocktail.

"You should have stayed," she says. "You should have known me."

———

At eight a.m. I can't call cardiology.

I know how to work a phone. I have fingers to dial, a mouth, an ear.

But I also have a daughter.

Both my sisters take that day off of work and hang out with me at Jess's. Katy brings over Jarmusch's *Only Lovers Left Alive*. It's a film about vampires, their alienation and disillusionment, citizens of a world that doesn't know they exist. They drive aimlessly around ruined Detroit. They wander the empty cobblestoned streets of Tangier. They need blood.

I don't tell my sisters about my confusion. I probably should. Keeping it a secret makes it worse, empowering these cravings, inflating their influence. I should be writing sonnets about rebirth! I should be rolling around in mud, praising Gaia for each and every creature on this striking, confusing planet!

Instead, I think only of the anesthesiologist running his needle into my artery, that brilliant shining bite from his fang.

———

Lelo and I get some time alone. We are at my sister's place, while Jess and Katy take Ava to a local park. We get to be husband and wife for a bit, before she goes home to do all the heavy lifting for our family, while I sit around, lie around, recuperating and harboring an eight ball of guilt while talking to an imaginary Nazi doctor.

I want to be someone else, somebody better. Someone who's never conversed with a duffel bag or a dying dog or Forssmann. But this is my little life, the only one I get, and I'm not going to let relapse run rampant, razing happiness.

That's what I keep telling myself. As I lie in Jess's guest room. In the shower. On walks. I say, "You don't matter anymore. It's Ava; it's all Ava."

Lelo sits next to me on the couch. She is, I believe, just happy that I'm still here, with a patched up heart. I am, I believe, primed for a run and need to tell her the truth.

"I want to get loaded," I say to Lelo.

"Okay."

"I need to go to a meeting."

"Now?"

"Soon."

"What can I do?" she asks.

"It's all I'm thinking about and that makes me hate myself."

"Don't."

"It feels impossible that I won't relapse."

"You won't."

"I might."

"No," she says, "you're not allowed."

I laugh, which is what she's trying to do.

"Drugs and drink and strokes and heart surgery," I say, "you should've picked a better husband."

"Leave my husband alone," she says.

———

When I was still hiding in 2½D, say two months out of rehab, one night Lelo and I watched *The Deer Hunter*. She was awake as it started but she nodded off before De Niro and Walken were shipped to Vietnam.

If you've never seen it, these American POWs are forced to play Russian roulette, sitting at a small table, holding a revolver to their heads and pulling the trigger. A lot of them shot themselves. One of their VC captors loved seeing these soldiers blow their own brains out and when he didn't think they were pulling the trigger quickly enough, he'd slap them in the face and scream, "*Di di mau!*" which means something like, "Hurry up," and these broken POWs could only be smacked so many times and could only hear, "*Di di mau!*" yelled inches from their ears before they'd do it, pulling that trigger, and some of them fell down dead and some of them survived—at least until their turn came again—and these men were terrified and wrecked but they didn't have a choice: At least if they played the game, there was the possibility that the gun's chamber would be empty, that the bullet wouldn't cut into their skulls, but if they refused to play, they had no hope.

And as I watched the movie, I cried. Not for these POWs. They were paid actors, handsome and rich and pretending to be busted in their souls. Their shellshock ended when the director said *cut*. I cried for all of us who weren't pretending. Those of us who played Russian roulette with booze and drugs. Those of us who pull the trigger and wonder whether the bullet will come. Those of us who hear, *"Di di mau!"* all the time, not just from other people, and not just from ourselves but from all sorts of inanimate objects. Bottles talking to us. Pipes, pills, needles. Every time we brave the outside world we play a sadistic game of Relapse Roulette. But we don't have a choice, can't stay in 2½D forever. We have to hold that gun to our head and see what happens.

———

I haven't really told you much about the stroke three years prior: That morning, I had been in a Los Feliz bungalow, checking email and was set to sit on a panel at the *Los Angeles Times* Festival of Books. This was before Ava was born. It was only Lelo and me. It had been an exhilarating weekend, filled with the camaraderie of other literary nerds and shortly, we were on our way to the festival.

A pop in my right temple, a noise like a match being extinguished in water. In some animal sense, I knew I was dying. I remember thinking: *This is the end of my life and what will I do with this final batch of seconds?*

I decided to spend them telling Lelo I loved her.

Wobbled into the bedroom where she was getting ready and

tried to say, "I love you," but my mouth didn't work, produced these macerated syllables that didn't mean anything and she said, "Are you okay?" and I thought, *What a way to go out, being misunderstood when trying to tell a woman you love her.*

———

My heart may not be technically defective any longer, yet there's a part of me that will always adore drugs. Those Sirens won't go away, and there are days I detest being sober, but it beats the alternative. Ava beats the alternative.

Our lives are always in flux, so many contradictions comprising our identities. Forssmann is a monster *and* a genius. We all are. We are never just one thing. I was never only the heart defect, only the author or junkie or husband or father or professor or drunk. I wear all these like layers of skin. Like stars creating a constellation.

———

Even our sun has a past. It takes eight minutes for its light to reach us, so every time we're warmed by its heat, we're living in the past.

———

I do finally end up at the *LA Times* Festival of Books, better late than never, a month after the surgery. I'm still so weak but that doesn't matter. I sit on stage with a few other writers, Lelo and Ava not far away. During the panel, I talk about art and parenthood and teaching and learning.

There is a placard in front of me with my name.

There is a bottle of water.

There is a microphone.

And there is a roomful of people, the audience a hundred strong. It isn't a stadium full of screaming fans, and it doesn't have to be. It's a moment in which I am surrounded by others who love literature the same way that I do.

My heart is fixed and it beats. And the three other writers on stage have beating hearts too, and everyone in the crowd has them.

We are all together.

10

IT'S HALLOWEEN, 8:08 P.M. IT'S BEEN SEVEN MONTHS since my surgery, the freelapse. Lelo and Ava are already asleep, done in by a maniacal trick or treat through the Mission. We had dressed up as the weather, the whole family a different "character." Ava was a snow flurry; Lelo, a rain cloud, ribbons of blue scarves cascading down her dress.

Me, I was lightning.

Here's how you look like lightning, according to Ava, our bossy art director: You wear a pink wig with lightning bolts painted on each cheek, clad in all black with a felt lightning bolt stitched to your t-shirt. That's how to make yourself look like lightning and you're welcome.

If you ask me, though, I looked like one of Ziggy Stardust's roadies, schlepping gear across the galaxy.

"I'm lightning," I said to Ava, once Lelo had forged both yellow bolts on my face, before we embarked on our sugar sojourn. "What do you think?"

She pondered my lightning-likeness, then shook her head. "No, you're Princess Daddy."

"I'm dressed like lightning, remember?"

"Princess Daddy," Ava said, patting my pink wig, which

meant, *I've made my decision and that's the end of it and from henceforth you'll be known as Princess Daddy and get that through your thick head, okay?*

Well, there you have it.

Halloween used to be whiskey and one-night stands, and now it's Princess Daddy, still with the lightning bolts tagged on his cheeks, all by his lonesome at 8:15, writing in the dark, sober on a Saturday night.

———

When a fifth-grader drinks it's often alone. It's often alone because he's often alone.

This is after the fifth-grader's dad leaves. After he's escaped to California. After he hosts the boy for a weekend every once in a while. So the mother works two jobs, one as a secretary, the other as a music director at a church. Which means she works way more than forty hours a week.

He's what they call a latchkey kid. Or that's what they were called in the '80s. Mom leaves money for pizzas. He orders Domino's because they deliver in half an hour or less. They have to be there in under thirty minutes or the pizza is free.

When the fifth-grader is not drinking alone, he drinks with his best friend, Brenty, who has his own story for why he likes to drink in elementary school but that's not for me to tell.

The fifth-grader gulps fuzzy navels or box wine. Depending on what's left over. It's easy for him to swipe box wine because the box isn't see-through. The mother has no idea the quantity, no idea how much she's had. The fuzzy navels are out of a blender. That's how she likes to drink them. Blended. Orange juice and peach schnapps. It makes sense to drink blended drinks in the desert because it's so hot. She'll always leave some in the blender. Sometimes it's just the dregs. Sometimes, it's half-full.

Regardless, the fifth-grader always finishes the slurpee. Finishes it and feels silly. He feels—if this makes any sense—important.

And when Brenty's over it's like New Year's Eve. They blast MTV. They sing along, dance, play air guitar. They watch basketball; they play basketball. They call girls. They swim in the pool. They play Nintendo. They call getting drunk getting *juiced*.

"I'm so juiced," one will say.

"We're juiced!" says the other.

When a delivery man rings the doorbell, the fifth-grader runs and says, "Hi!" and the delivery guy says, "Large pepperoni, right?" and the fifth-grader says, "How are you?" and the delivery guy says, "$9.99," and the fifth-grader says, "Are you hungry?"

They are never hungry.

And this isn't just about a fifth-grader. It's about a fourth-grader. A sixth-grader. There's so much box wine back then. So many blender-dregs that the boy can fill that swimming pool in the backyard.

Sometimes feeling important lasts for hours, drink after drink, the fifth-grader having the time of his life. He likes being drunk. Likes being dizzy and clumsy and silly and slurring his words. One night, Brenty watches the fifth-grader shit his pants, and this important fifth-grader just stands there laughing about it, laughing his head off, and his eyes cry 'cause this is funny, so fucking funny, the fifth-grader feeling happy with shit in his pants.

It only happens once, but he does get a free pizza. It takes the delivery guy something like thirty-three minutes to get there. The boy can hear him screech up out front and slam the car's door and run over the gravel in the front yard and ring the bell and the boy enjoys the sounds of somebody rushing to be with him.

"Sorry, I'm late," the delivery man says. "The pizza's on the house."

"It's cool," says the fifth-grader, drunk and important.

———

No one ever told me the truth. I didn't know the real reason my dad left me in the desert with my mom until after he died.

For years, I'd carried this desolate question around: Why would he leave me behind? If he had to go, why didn't he take me with him?

The truth was simple. The truth was self-preservation: The minister was getting run out of town for screwing a woman in his parish, and if there was a custody battle with my mom, his secret would come out. If he left quietly, no one had to know.

So he saved himself, moved to Berkeley, and started over.

Giving my mom full custody.

Giving him a cover story.

My father loved me—I have to believe that—but he loved himself a little bit more.

I want to write something judgmental. I want to write how as a father myself now I'm appalled, say something about how I'd never treat my daughter that way, and I hope that's true, but you never really know, I guess. You don't know if you're capable of acting selflessly until everything ruptures around you.

It wasn't until after his funeral that my biological mom told me the truth about his affair in Arizona, telling me it wasn't the first time, either.

I said, "Why are you telling me this now, after he's dead? I can't ask his side."

"I was always hoping he'd tell you himself," she said.

"What am I supposed to do with this?"

"It's your life," she said. "You're supposed to know about it."

But the more I found out, the less I knew. And the fact that he was dead made this so harrowing. All these questions and I'd never know the answers. I wanted to hear his whole side.

Wanted to know every fleck of detail. Wanted to lay in the crannies of each decision he ever made about me, but I'll never get to do that. I'll have to endure never knowing.

And he had to endure the malignant opposite: He had to live his whole life knowing exactly what he'd done.

If it was going to happen—if he was ever tempted to confess the truth to me—it was probably during that moment before my wedding to Blue. When he and I were putting on our rented tuxedos. When his hands shook so violently that he couldn't get his shirt buttoned up. When I dressed him like he had dressed me as a baby, a toddler, before leaving.

The two of us, father and son, both miraculous liars, face to face as I worked his buttons. I know he wanted to say, "It wasn't that I didn't love you. That's not why I left you there."

"Then why?"

"It's not simple."

"But why?"

"I'd do it differently now."

"But why?"

"I just... I did... I thought I made the right decision at the time."

And I'd say, "But she was sick."

And he'd say, "I'm sorry."

And I'd say, "But didn't you love me?"

And he'd say, "I'm sorry."

And I'd say, "But didn't you want to protect me?"

And he'd say, "I'm sorry."

And I'd say, "But..."

Really, there would be nothing else to ask. I've spent so much of my life wondering *why*, and yet that's not the right question. Most of life is just a boiled paste of *what*, a pulp of stewed facts. This is what happened. Period.

Of course, as we finished getting on our rented tuxedos, he chose not to be honest with me, even as he only had a few weeks left alive. Of course, I chose not to be honest with him about booze and drugs, and I had years still, but I was so scared of him knowing me—what I considered the *real* me, liquored up with a cocaine halo, a syringe of special K crammed in my tricep.

There we were, two men who cherished blind spots. We loved each other and barely knew each other and there's no reason to drag *why* into this. Let's leave it at the pulpy *what*. A son buttoning his father's rented shirt…

———

I came across an article written by one of Forssmann's daughters—he actually had six children. The piece was published after he was dead. Her conclusions were all wrong, contorted with loyalty, lighting fact on fire.

She defended her father's affiliation with the Nazis, finessing his involvement, making him sound like some passive victim of the political tumult of Germany in the early 1930s. "Forssmann followed the tide and joined the National Socialist Party…" she wrote of her father, making the thesis of her piece that he was, what, just going with the flow, hanging with the cool kids?

I get it. It's her dad.

But he joined the Nazi party in 1932—a year before Hitler became chancellor—and Forssmann stayed a member until 1945, when he was put in an American POW camp.

This isn't about whether he was an anti-Semite; this is about his daughter. I'm talking about children sifting through the detritus of our parents' existences looking for meaning, for purpose. For a narrative.

Love sullies history.

It makes us too literal.

Love makes us incompatible with complexity.

Like in my own life: I'd always believed my mom was *bad*

because she left the fifth-grader alone. My dad was *good*, the enlightened minister.

Binary: one good, one bad.

But that's pat, useless, wrong.

Now, with a kid of my own, with a drinking and drug problem of my own as well, my assignments have muddled. My mother is a *good* person, one who didn't have a clear head back then. My father was *bad* because he did have lucid faculties, and he used them to abandon me.

Maybe I'd feel differently if he trusted me enough for honesty. I wonder how that talk would have gone. Would it have changed my life? Would it have changed his? How would it have been presented to me? Would I have gotten contrition or defensiveness? Would he brush his behavior aside, roll out rickety excuses? And what would two liars like us have done with the truth anyway?

Though it's hard to see the shimmers of complexity in my life, I can see it for Forssmann; in his, I recognize it effortlessly, like seeing a fly, a flower, a swastika. For Forssmann, I can see him having to talk to all of his children about being a Nazi, each conversation crackling with a unique reaction.

With at least one of his kids, it had to happen like this: An incensed child, now grown, fighting the impulse to strike the old man, stopping a fist from hitting the father's deceitful face.

"You were a Nazi?" the grown child says.

"It's not that simple," says Forssmann.

"You were a Nazi?"

"Yes and no."

"You were a Nazi," the grown child says, changing the punctuation on so much more than the ending of his sentence, never talking to the father again.

With another Forssmann progeny, it's simple: The kid, laying a head in the father's lap, says, "I don't care what you did. You are my father and I love you. No matter what, I love you, Papa."

Another reacts with a cluster of, "No no no no no no," and Forssmann says, "Listen, please, so I can make you understand, please, listen to me," and the grown child says again, "No no no no no no," and Forssmann begs, "Please, listen," but the grown child is surrounded with a wall, an electric fence, a penitentiary of *no no nos* that can't be penetrated. No one will get in.

And with another: The sobs dismantle the words, the grown kid coughing up thoughts too garbled to mean much, but still the child tries to speak, massive torrents of futile sounds.

Forssmann, unable to decipher them, says, "I can't understand you."

To which the grown child unleashes another set of molested hysterics.

"I can't understand you," the father says again.

The kid conjures a quick calm, one that won't be sustained, something makeshift and temporary, only to say, "We can't understand each other; I'll never understand you again."

Then there's the grown child who has a seed of sinister sympathy growing inside. This kid saying to the father, "If only we'd won the war…"

Finally, there's the last grown child, who doesn't react with anger or pathos or stupefied confusion or understanding. This one looks at the father and refuses to give him a single tear, a whelp, won't offer up one puff of dialogue. Because it's happened, frozen, marring human history, all that's left for this grown child to do is be better than the father.

Forssmann penned his autobiography, *Experiments on Myself*, late in life, in which he argued that his allegiance to the Nazis was only camouflage, and that from the inside he was able to help people, though I don't buy that because as a surgeon during the war, he operated on soldiers, patching them up so they could keep fighting, so they could win the war and spread the plague of their ethos.

As I'm writing, I find myself thinking this: *Argue it any way you want, Werner, you were a Nazi, not for your whole life, but that's who you were during those thirteen years, and you have to own it. We always have to own it.*

One minute, I'm alone at the kitchen table, still wearing my lightning costume, and then Forssmann storms in. He doesn't look good. He's pale. He's wheezing. He's wet. His lab coat is the color of street snow.

"Why are you wet?" I say.

"I swam," he says.

"You swam here?"

"When I was about to be captured," he says, "we were outside Leningrad. I swam across the river to be captured by Americans, instead of the Russians. They would have killed me."

Forssmann shivers, sneezes into his hand, wipes it on the wet coat.

"We were on the Russian front," he says, "and the river was freezing, but I could choose my captors. I chose to live."

"Did your daughter know the truth about you before writing that article?"

"I often wonder: Did I make the right choice? Should I have let myself be killed by the Russians?"

"Did she know?" I say.

"Why are you dressed like that?" he says, motioning to my pink wig.

"Answer my question."

"Did she know what?"

"What you did."

"What did I do?"

"When you were a Nazi."

"She knows me."

"What does that mean?"

"She knows me."

"That's not good enough."

"She knows me!" he says.

Ava will know me, too. I'm making sure of that. I'm publishing my Nazi dissertation right here. She'll see my *Check Out Time*. She'll see me hurt that man at Coit Tower. She'll wince at my existence.

And weirdly, that doesn't make me hesitate to let this book out into the wild. Every page here has been a love letter to Ava. It might seem an odd one, considering all these dubious confessions, but that's what makes it a REAL love letter!

Forssmann reaches out to rip the wig off my head but I duck from his grip, and he says to me, "Who are you to judge?" and I say, "I read her bullshit article and she's just covering your tracks," and he says, "Will Ava cover yours?" and I say, "We're talking about you," and he says, "We've never been talking about me," and I say, "She doesn't have to," and he says, "But will she?" and I say, "I hope not," and he says, "But will she?" and I think about Ava writing an article, just like Forssmann's daughter, trying to make sense of my sprawling mistakes.

What I'm doing here is the exact opposite of Forssmann's daughter, who sought to protect and build back up her father's name. I'm tarnishing my father's reputation. Is this the right thing to do? Probably not. I only know that it's impossible to tell my story without telling some of his. He shouldn't have had affairs and he shouldn't have left me, saving himself by fleeing to California like Forssmann swimming the frigid river.

But on most fronts, he was a solid father. I have to give him that. He taught me many things. To fish. To gut a fish. Hell, he taught me countless other things but right now, for whatever reason, all I can recall is an image of us in a fishing boat.

We are on Lake Almanor. I am in my early twenties. It's five in the morning. We're drinking coffee. Once the sun comes up he'll crack two beers. My father isn't a heavy drinker. Certainly not in the morning, but fishing boats don't abide by the rules of the real world, apparently. Fathers and sons drink beers as the sun comes up and everything's fine.

I snag my line. I'm always doing that. I'm always snagging my line on an underwater log or a rock or lost anchor. He takes my pole, tries to jimmy the line free. It never works.

"Here," he says, handing me his pole, taking mine.

"I can fix it," I say.

"No, you can't," he says.

He's right. I am a shitty fisherman. He uses his teeth to bite through the line. He gets out his tackle box. He gets a fresh hook. He fastens it to the line with a complicated knot. He baits the hook. He casts. He cracks those beers.

He's smiling. We both are.

"I budget time to fix all your snags," he says.

Everybody at one time or another has to confront the fact our parents have more in common with convicts than martyrs. Some get literally locked up, like Kae, like Forssmann, while most of us stew in private incarcerations.

We have courtrooms in our heads.

The only jury that matters lives in your skull.

11

WRITING ABOUT RELAPSE ROULETTE REMINDS ME
of this time back in the late '90s, working at a French restaurant
on Valencia Street that's since turned over half-dozen times, and
after one shift or another, a bunch of us stayed to sit in the basement, drinking beers and blowing rails.

This happened at least once a month, sticking around from
midnight to six or seven in the morning, staggering out into the
sunshine with our stampeding cocaine hangovers, pulling these
tiny pellet-scabs from our noses that looked like watermelon
seeds.

There was a revolving crew who participated in these all-
nighters, but a few of us had perfect attendance: A busboy
named Angel who sold the drugs, the executive chef, and
another guy who tended bar with me, Shamus.

On this night, Angel brought along his cousin, who we were
informed before he got there was Angel's supplier. He was coming to give away some product, say thanks for all the grams we'd
been buying. His coke was good and we were all excited to meet
him, in the name of hitting it off and our newfound camaraderie leading to future price breaks on bindles. Of course, it never

worked that way, but we held out hope, if that word makes any sense in this context.

There were eight of us, give or take, crowded in a small basement office. Angel's cousin shook all our hands upon arriving, a slick-looking Mayan who wore a designer suit while the rest of us sat around in dirty t-shirts, Ben Davis pants, combat boots—a clog of nappy dudes listening to Minor Threat and burning through a case of Shiner.

I can't remember our guest of honor's name so let's call him Javier. He pulled out two cue balls of cocaine. He distributed a few razor blades, and we chipped pieces off these cue balls, rowing them up, until the table looked like a Google Earth shot of a farm, crops lined up straight and immaculate and ripe, ready to feed people's hungers.

The next few hours we feasted on these crops, time a blur of beers and rips and bad jokes. Shamus blowing his nose into a bar napkin and saying, "There goes twenty bucks!" and all of us sitting in this circle, laughing, even Javier.

We played records by the Misfits, Op Ivy, Fang, Bad Brains, SLF, NoMeansNo, Neurosis, the DKs, and a hundred others. We opened another case of beer. The room was hot boxed by spliffs. A flask of whiskey magically appeared. It was a party and we were happy.

But by four a.m. we were all totaled, too gakked, too bent up to drive ahead, though none of us would admit that. When it was our turn for a new line, we feigned enthusiasm, sucking up another rip and hoping our hearts would keep working.

On Shamus's next turn, he said, "I'm passing."

This gave us a gust of energy. "You're passing?"

"I can't do anymore."

"You're passing?"

"My nose isn't working."

"Passing is for suckers."

"I don't care what you guys say," he said, sitting there, folding his arms.

We were teasing, was all. Everything coming from our mouths was in good spirits. Like I said, we were all sideways wasted, but rules were rules and nobody bolted till we'd sucked up everything. That was how this worked.

But if he passed, that meant more for us.

Even if we didn't want more, we'd do it. That was how this worked, too.

So we'd all got our digs in on Shamus, and now we'd keep the circle going, each of us holding dollars to our noses and doing our lines, Shamus's lines.

Punk rock still cranking. Cigarettes lit on the butts of others. Still sitting in a circle around that table. The room reeking of body odor. We were ready to keep blowing rips, except here was when Javier barked something at Angel in Spanish.

Angel barked back.

Javier's face going red.

The chef, a white dude, spoke Spanish, too, and he followed the conversation with his eyes bouncing between them.

Javier rocketing to his feet.

Chair falling over.

Javier barking again.

Javier stomping his foot to accent his words.

Angel, still sitting, hollering back at him.

The chef's eye popping between them.

Javier screaming at his cousin. Poking him in the shoulder.

Angel averting his eyes to the floor.

Angel acquiescing.

Angel whispering something to his cousin.

Javier pacing back and forth.

Javier screaming still.

Us all sitting there. Not even ashing our cigarettes. Not even drinking our beers.

The chef saying to Shamus, "Do the line."

"I can't," said Shamus.

Javier said something else to Angel in Spanish, really calm this time, which made it even worse for us, even creepier, hearing Javier all collected.

Angel said something back. Angel said something that ended with, "*Por favor,*" and we knew what that meant and we didn't understand how *please* belonged in this basement.

"Just do the line," the chef said to Shamus.

"I can't."

"You have to."

"Sorry," said Shamus, his arms still crossed.

Javier lost his shit again, pacing and yelling and we just sat there with our rolled-up dollar bills. There might have been music playing at that point: It probably was. But I don't remember. All I know is in my memory—at this point—the volume on the Spanish conversation cranked louder and louder, Javier walking faster and faster, circling the table, circling all of us, talking to Angel in huffs and screams, and all of these words I didn't know the meaning of amping until they were the only sound in the world.

"What's up?" I said to Angel.

He waved me off. Angel and I were friends. We ate menudo and drank Dos Equis together before work sometimes, so when he didn't answer me I knew we were headed to hell.

"I'll do his," I said, pointing at Shamus. "I'll do it, Javier. *Está bien.*"

"No!" Javier said.

"*Está bien,*" I said again.

Mimicking my terrible Spanish accent, he said, "It's not *está* fucking *bien!*"

"I'm not trying to be a dick," Shamus said to Javier. "I'm wrecked, man."

That was when the gun came out. One second, none of us

knew it was in the room, stowed away in his tailored suit, and soon it was in his hand with an arm extending toward the table. Javier storming over to Shamus and putting it right against his head. Shamus shutting his eyes. Shamus's shoulders scrunching up. Shamus balling his hands and resting them on the table. Shamus gritting his teeth.

"Holy shit!" we said.

"What the fuck?" we said.

All of us looking at Angel. All of us expecting Angel to do something. But he just stared at his cousin, not saying anything.

Javier holding the gun to Shamus's temple.

Shamus's lips moving a bit. Probably praying.

"I give you free *bolsa*," Javier said, so calm, "you do it all."

We knew the word *bolsa* because that was what Angel called his little plastic bags of coke. *Bolsa* didn't feel right for cue balls.

Javier bouncing the gun softly off Shamus's skin.

"Okay," Shamus said.

"I'm sorry," Shamus said.

"I'll do it," Shamus said.

The gun grazing his temple. Shamus leaned over and blew his bump. Javier put the gun back in his suit. Simple as that. He said, "There. Now *está bien*."

He righted his chair and sat back down at the table. Smiling, making eye contact with the rest of us. A look like: Let's go on as if nothing happened. A look like: Continue, friends.

From there, the night became a race, trying to do the drugs as fast as we could so leaving wouldn't mean a gun to our own heads. If all these lines were in fact crops, we had to eat everything in a hurry before it all went rotten, before everything spoiled.

I quit that job soon after, not because of the night with the gun, but jumped ship to a new restaurant a couple blocks down, at the corner of 22nd and Valencia. I lost touch with that whole crew and hadn't thought of that night in years, until today.

Ava loves birds and wakes us up about 5:30 in the morning, wanting to look across the street to a church, pigeons and tweet-ies perched on the steeple, some pacing back and forth. Ava watches them for twenty minutes without squirming on my lap, and sitting still for that long is unusual for her. I cherish these moments of snuggled stillness.

"What's in your mouth?" I ask her.

"Gum."

"Where'd you get gum?"

"My nose," she says.

It's the hardest she's ever made me laugh; I hug her, kiss the top of her head.

It scares me so much that she relies on me to survive. Relies on the dirty-laundry leper. The quantum leaper. The alcoholic car jacker. One of the Jims. The winner with his stolen money. The criminal. The caveman. The check-out timer.

All those deranged, dislocated days. All those curious masks, living inside me like backwash in a bottle. And I'm in charge of keeping someone safe? How? Why?

Because of her fondness for birds, Lelo and I take her to the zoo, thinking she'll love the African aviary, but she's not impressed, barely giving any of the exotic birds the once-over. She does giggle and coo at a pigeon playing in a dirty puddle by the monkeys. She lacks sophistication when it comes to birds.

We stand in line getting hot dogs at a concession stand, next to a crazy big playground filled with ecstatic, shrieking kids. I notice the guy bussing tables. He looks familiar, though I can't place him right off.

His hair is gray. So is his skin. I keep double-, triple-taking him behind my sunglasses, and that's when I recognize Shamus.

He's not wearing these fifteen years well, rotund around the middle, more hunched than I remember him being. He has a rag in his hand and there are plenty of tables that need to be wiped down, but he ambles between them, not really doing much. He wasn't a very good bartender back in the day, either, but he was always a great guy. I felt all right working extra hard doing a shift with Shamus because we laughed so much during the night.

"Don't look," I say to Lelo, "but that busboy used to be one of my drinking buddies."

Of course, she looks. He doesn't notice, surveying a dirty table before doing nothing about it and moving on to survey the next mess. The rag looks like a prop in his hand.

I feel bad for Shamus, feel embarrassed for him. If I was bussing tables at the god damn zoo the last thing I'd want was some wise ass from my past waving his daughter and wife in my face.

"He was a good dude," I say to Lelo.

"He's not dead," she says.

While I pay for the hot dogs, while all those children writhe around the playground making their own animal noises, Lelo and Ava find a spot to sit.

Shamus still stands on the edge of all the dirty tables, hoping they might clean themselves. That rag is pristine.

I'm over-thinking this. Just go say hi.

"Shamus," I say, walking up to him and tossing my hand out for a shake.

He looks at me like we don't know each other.

"Josh Mohr," I say.

He still has no idea.

"Josh Mohr," I say, "from Three Ring."

He moves the prop rag to his left hand and smiles at me. "Josh!"

"Shamus!"

Our handshake evolves into a monster hug.

Then we bullshit like it's the old days, fall into an easy rapport because why shouldn't we? There were hours, many hours when it was just the two of us, before work or after, unloading the liquor delivery, counting the till, blowing bindles, shooting bourbon.

One night, he even warned me to stay away from needles, knowing how much special K I'd been shooting. "Be careful," he said. "That shit can cripple your life."

"I'm fine."

"You're fine until you're not," he said.

He was right. He is right. K can mash you.

But so can booze. And standing next to Shamus at the zoo, it's clear he's been going at it pretty hard. Not only can I smell the alcohol on him, I can see it, skin zombied out and plumped with water weight.

We talk about this person from Three Ring and that one, and did you hear about so and so? We laugh, talking about all the servers and food runners I screwed.

"I was always jealous of your conquests," he says, "but I got one too. Tracey. Remember her?"

"I left one for you because I care."

"Glad to see you're still a dick."

"Hold on," I say, "I want to introduce you to somebody."

I run over and swipe Ava from Lelo, ask my wife to follow me.

The throng of kids swarming that playground.

Animal noises in the distance.

Pretty soon, I thrust Ava at Shamus.

He puts his pristine rag up, blocking the baby. "I'm not good with kids."

"She's easy," I say.

"You keep her," says Shamus.

I do. It's a couple minutes of small talk, introducing my wife and daughter to him. We make phony claims to track each other down for coffee or lunch. We're both lying and both know it, but it doesn't matter.

I don't know if he felt uncomfortable or not—maybe he doesn't care that he's working at the zoo. But I feel uncomfortable for him. I wonder if that rag could wipe away some of his decisions. Would he want that? Or is he happy living at a table still stacked with empty bottles?

I'm not saying any of this to make fun of Shamus. Far from it. Point is I could be Shamus and he could be me, or either of us could have gotten shot in that basement or died in any of a thousand asinine alcoholic ways.

One wrong fistfight, one wrong needle, one too many *bolsas*, a freelapse, one more lonely night than any human can handle and soon you're on the Golden Gate, sobbing and wondering if the answer's at the bottom of the ocean.

It's not, of course. But you endure too much electric shame and you'll imbibe on any antidote. I'm not safe from that fate. In fact, I can relapse before you finish this page. That chance lurks in all our lives, though. A diagnosis. A car accident. Heart attacks. Lightning strikes. Whiskey shots. Whatever.

But so far I haven't relapsed again.

And so far is all I've got.

Two Dollar Radio
Books too loud to Ignore

Two Dollar Radio
Books too loud to Ignore

ALSO AVAILABLE Here are some other titles you might want to dig into.

THE ONLY ONES NOVEL BY CAROLA DIBBELL

⇢ **Best Books 2015:** *Washington Post, O, The Oprah Magazine,* NPR

← "Breathtaking." —NPR

INEZ WANDERS A POST-PANDEMIC world immune to disease. Her life is altered when a grief-stricken mother that hired her to provide genetic material backs out, leaving Inez with the product: a baby girl.

BINARY STAR NOVEL BY SARAH GERARD

⇢ **Los Angeles Times Book Prize Finalist**

⇢ **Best Books 2015:** *BuzzFeed, Vanity Fair,* NPR

← "Rhythmic, hallucinatory, yet vivid as crystal." —NPR

AN ELEGIAC, INTENSE PORTRAIT of two young lovers as they battle their personal afflictions while on a road trip across the U.S.

THE REACTIVE NOVEL BY MASANDE NTSHANGA

← "Often teems with a beauty that seems to carry on in front of its glue-huffing wasters despite themselves." —*Slate*

A CLEAR-EYED, COMPASSIONATE ACCOUNT of a young HIV+ man grappling with the sudden death of his brother in South Africa.

THE GLOAMING NOVEL BY MELANIE FINN

← "Deeply satisfying. [*The Gloaming*] deserves major attention." —*New York Times Book Review*

AFTER AN ACCIDENT LEAVES her estranged in a Swiss town, Pilgrim Jones absconds to east Africa, settling in a Tanzanian outpost where she can't shake the unsettling feeling that she's being followed.

Thank you for supporting independent culture!
Feel good about yourself.

Books to read!

Now available at **TWODOLLARRADIO.com** or your favorite bookseller.

MIRA CORPORA NOVEL BY JEFF JACKSON

⇢ **Los Angeles Times Book Prize Finalist**

⇠ "A piercing howl of a book." —*Slate*

A COMING OF AGE story for people who hate coming of age stories, featuring a colony of outcast children, teenage oracles, amusement parks haunted by gibbons, and mysterious cassette tapes.

NOG NOVEL BY RUDOLPH WURLITZER

⇠ "[*Nog*'s] combo of Samuel Beckett syntax and hippie-era freakiness mapped out new literary territory for generations to come." —*Time Out New York*

NOG TELLS THE TALE of a man adrift through the American West, armed with nothing more than his own three pencil-thin memories and an octopus in a bathysphere.

THE ORANGE EATS CREEPS
NOVEL BY GRACE KRILANOVICH

⇢ **National Book Foundation '5 Under 35' Award**

⇠ "Breathless, scary, and like nothing I've ever read." —NPR

A RUNAWAY SEARCHES FOR her disappeared foster sister along the "Highway That Eats People" haunted by a serial killer named Dactyl.

SQUARE WAVE NOVEL BY MARK DE SILVA

⇠ "Compelling and horrifying." —*Chicago Tribune*

A GRAND NOVEL OF ideas and compelling crime mystery, about security states past and present, weather modification science, micro-tonal music, and imperial influences.

SOME RECOMMENDED LOCATIONS FOR READING TWO DOLLAR RADIO BOOKS:

Elevated places, such as hilltops or vineyards. Cafés and wine bars with high spirits. Double-decker buses, planes, hot air balloons, and trees. Or, pretty much anywhere because books are portable and the perfect technology!